BEYOND POVERTY AND

D0355575

Beyond Poverty and Affluence argues that, like a virus that has developed an immunity to the cure, poverty, environmental degeneration, and unemployment successfully resist the remedy of growth in industrial production. Bob Goudzwaard and Harry de Lange maintain that over the last several decades the solutions attempted by industrialized nations either have not helped or have dramatically exacerbated these problems, which have become structural features of contemporary economies. The authors propose as an alternative an 'economics of care' and offer a twelve-step program for economic recovery in Canada.

Goudzwaard and de Lange contend that poverty, environmental damage, and unemployment have a common origin – namely, structural flaws in classical and contemporary neoclassical economic thought, including that of Adam Smith and Karl Marx. Drawing on the ideas of thinkers as diverse as René Girard and Hannah Arendt, on numerous Canadian sources, and on their own Christian tradition, the authors propose a 'pre-care' economy, which places 'care' needs first and only then addresses the scope of production, in contrast to a 'post-care' economy, which pursues maximum consumption and production. The authors also describe in detail the structural changes that the Canadian economy would have to undergo in order to become a pre-care economy.

The authors' proposals deal with such issues as international currency creation, the environment, labour/management relations, the funding of social programs, the scope of production and technological development, the structure of economic decision-making, and the dropping of trade barriers in North America and Europe.

BOB GOUDZWAARD, a former member of the Dutch parliament, is Professor of Economics and Social Philosophy at the Free University of Amsterdam. He is a consultant for Citizens for Public Justice, a Canada-wide advocacy organization, and author of several books.

HARRY DE LANGE is Professor Emeritus of Economics at the University of Utrecht. He was for many years president of Holland's highest-profile Development Cooperation Agency and has published widely on economics and social justice.

Beyond Poverty and Affluence

Towards a Canadian Economy of Care

Bob Goudzwaard and Harry de Lange

With a Foreword by Maurice F. Strong
Secretary-General of the 1992 Earth Summit
Chairman of Ontario Hydro

Translated and Edited by
Mark R. Vander Vennen

UNIVERSITY OF TORONTO PRESS
Toronto Buffalo London

© Bob Goudzwaard and Harry de Lange 1994
English translation © Mark R. Vander Vennen 1994
Published by University of Toronto Press Incorporated 1995
Toronto Buffalo London

This book is a translation and adaptation of the third, revised and expanded
edition of *Genoeg van te Veel, Genoeg van te Weinig; Wissels omzetten in de
economie* (Baarn: Ten Have 1986/1991).

Printed in Canada

ISBN 0-8020-7637-8

∞

Printed on acid-free paper

Canadian Cataloguing in Publication Data

Goudzwaard, B.
    Beyond poverty and affluence : towards a
    Canadian economy of care

    Translation of: Genoeg van te Veel, Genoeg van te Weinig.
    Includes bibliographical references and index.
    ISBN 0-8020-7637-8

    1. Canada – Economic policy – 1991– .*
    I. Lange, H. M. de. II. Title.

HD87.G6813 1995   338.971   C95-930178-X

University of Toronto Press acknowledges the financial assistance to its
publishing program of the Canada Council and the Ontario Arts Council.

Contents

Foreword

By Maurice F. Strong

The Earth Summit has concentrated the mind wonderfully on these issues.

World Link
Magazine of the World Economic Forum

This borrowing from Dr Samuel Johnson was especially appropriate in describing the United Nations Conference on Environment and Development (UNCED) at Rio de Janeiro in June 1992. The gathering concentrated not only the mind, but also the hearts, of humankind. It riveted the world's attention on the fragility of Earth's environment and the finiteness of its resources. It illuminated, as never before, in the presence of the largest host of the world's political leaders ever gathered in one place, the indisputable fact that the global community is on a pathway to destruction.

The full quotation from Dr Johnson is this: 'When a man knows he is to be hanged in a fortnight, it concentrates his mind wonderfully.' And though the Earth Summit was not convened under quite such exigent circumstances, it was nevertheless steeped in a sense of urgency and ultimatum. There was a pervasive conviction that if agreement was not achieved, at least in principle, to set in Rio a new, more sustainable, more secure, and more humane course for Planet Earth and its inhabitants, there would be few better chances.

Thus the minds at Rio were concentrated wonderfully – and the critical agreement was reached. It did not go as far as many wanted. Prime Minister Gro Harlem Brundtland, chair of the United Nations

World Commission on Environment and Development, whose prescient report, *Our Common Future*, was a precursor to the Earth Summit, summed up Rio this way: 'Progress in many fields, too little progress in most fields, and no progress at all in some fields.' But, she added: 'I am convinced that we will succeed in standing up to the dangers facing us because there are simply no alternatives.'

The Earth Summit was neither a beginning nor an end, and it most assuredly was not a 'one-shot' panacea. Certainly the short-term signs of real action are not encouraging. Since Rio, there has been an understandable, albeit regrettable, tendency to lapse back to business as usual, particularly in light of the pressing political and economic concerns that have gripped the world. It would not be realistic to expect the kind of fundamental changes called for at the conference to emerge quickly or easily.

But there is real basis for hope that the UNCED has laid the foundations for the changes in public attitudes and the political mind-set necessary to achieve the transition to sustainable development.

The spirit of Rio burns on undiminished. Indeed, the Earth Summit has produced a universal dialogue of unheard-of intensity and resolve. The protocols achieved there, along with the *Agenda 21* implementation blueprint, are on everyone's agenda, at every level of society and in every corner of the Earth. The issue of sustainable development, which languished as an abstruse and idealistic notion for five years after it was propounded in the Brundtland Report in 1987, now blossomed full-force as an inescapable and crucial imperative.

It is clear that, while governments may be approaching sustainable development with characteristic wariness, ordinary people, in communities and special-interest organizations around the world, are not about to let the spirit of Rio die on the vine. They are translating it into a new era of grassroots interest and action that will further implementation of *Agenda 21* and infuse the political process with new energies and fresh resolve.

And that 'wonderful' concentration of minds has, among other things, resulted in a concentration of wonderful minds – as indeed befits a subject of such compelling significance. Among these are Bob Goudzwaard and Harry de Lange, two eminent and probing Dutch economists who bring to the subject an engaging mix of academic empiricism, perceptive practicality, and moral responsibility. My own sense of the human dimension of sustainable development was heightened immeasurably by my 14-year association with Dr de Lange on the

Working Committee on Church and Society of the World Council of Churches.

This book, *Beyond Poverty and Affluence*, is the long-overdue English translation and North American adaptation of the third edition of the authors' work, the first edition of which appeared in 1986. The third edition was also translated and published in German. It was translated into English and edited into two editions, with this one primarily for a Canadian audience, by my esteemed friend Mark Vander Vennen. I commend both of these editions to English-language readers everywhere.

Preface

This book, *Beyond Poverty and Affluence*, first surfaced in Dutch in 1986. The impetus for writing it was our conviction that currently accepted economic practice could not aid in the renewal of society. Events in the intervening years have in no way weakened this conviction. On the contrary, now more than ever, we believe, industrialized societies in North America and Europe must grapple with several distressing issues: poverty, which is spreading like a cancer in many areas of the world; ominous forms of pollution and environmental degradation; and on-going losses in both the quantity and quality of work. Together these realities demand reflection and bold new economic practice.

After several years of dialogue, in 1986 we published our reflections and proposals jointly. In 1990, a German translation and edition of the book appeared, which is now used in discussion groups, especially in eastern Germany. In 1991, a third, revised and expanded Dutch edition was published. In 1995, an 'international' English edition was published simultaneously in the United States and in Europe. Now, in view of a Canadian audience, further revisions have been made.

We are delighted that a number of Canadians, too numerous to mention by name, have supplied most of the domestic aspects of the book. This edition has therefore had substantial Canadian input, which was an essential requirement for us. Many of these contributors – to whom we are deeply indebted – are associated with Citizens for Public Justice,* a national organization of Canadian citizens headquartered in Toronto. This interchange has confirmed our experience that transatlan-

*Citizens for Public Justice, 229 College Street, Toronto, Ontario, M5T 1R4; phone: (416) 979-2443.

tic cross-fertilization of ideas holds considerable promise. Not long ago, for example, in a meeting between the European churches and the Commission of the European Union, the churches of Europe drew the attention of the commission and its staff to several outstanding proposals made by Douglas Roche, Canada's distinguished former ambassador for disarmament at the United Nations.[1]

We offer our deliberations in the hope that interested Canadians – persons and groups as well as our colleagues in economics – will respond with constructive criticisms. We also trust that they will, where necessary, improve the proposals for economic recovery outlined below. We have drafted these proposals in the hope that a public consensus will emerge not only in Canada but also in all of the industrialized nations, which holds our eyes and ears wide open to the needs of the developing countries, especially to those of the poor living there, and to the interests of future generations.

The twelve-step program for economic recovery proposed in the final chapter demonstrates how alternative reflection about today's economy can take concrete shape. The steps framed there also contain elements of proposals made by other organizations and research bodies. We present them in the hope that the public will exert stronger pressure on politicians and institutions to begin to implement these and similar proposed steps.

Before we begin, a word is in order about our personal context. Throughout the book, we argue that the foundations of today's local and international economy require renewal. In this, we have been influenced by the exchange of ideas on social ethics occurring within the ecumenical community. Both of us are members of Christian churches in the Netherlands and serve on the Working Group on Church and Society of the Dutch Council of Churches. The ecumenical world is attempting to link more closely a personal and collective faith commitment with the day-to-day activities of those who profess that faith, not only socially and culturally, but also economically. Those working in the ecumenical context have also subjected their reflections to theoretical scrutiny, recognizing, for example, that the specific concept of justice that they adopt will have a marked effect on whatever efforts they may make to promote justice in an often unjust world.

Finally, we wish to reiterate publicly our heartfelt gratitude to the many friends in Canada whose efforts have led to the publication of this edition. We especially wish to thank Maurice Strong for his most gracious contribution of the book's Foreword. We also particularly wish to thank Gerald Vandezande, who kindly read the English text and offered valuable suggestions, and Mark Vander Vennen, our translator and editor. Not only has Mark translated and edited the 'international' English edition of the book, but he has also spearheaded the Canadian research and edited this edition. He deserves an award for his patience and endurance!

BEYOND POVERTY AND AFFLUENCE:

Towards a Canadian Economy of Care

Introduction

In this book, we attempt to demonstrate that the Canadian economy, as part of the industrialized world, has reached the point where it must be fundamentally renewed. We argue that the industrialized economies, in both theory and practice, are incapable of resolving the major economic dilemmas of our time – poverty, environmental degradation, and unemployment. We suggest that these problems call for a new economic agenda. We also explore the prospects of finding a genuine resolution to these difficulties, a resolution that lies beyond the grasp of today's commonly accepted solutions. And this process leads us to recommend, at the book's conclusion, a twelve-step program for economic recovery in Canada.

This book arises out of a specific observation. In our experience, the large majority of our economist colleagues and politicians defend the position that, if we can restore growth in industrial production, then we can solve several of the distressing problems plaguing today's national and international economies. More precisely, they argue that a restoration of growth in industrial production will remedy poverty, environmental degeneration, and unemployment. In our view, however, this approach is thoroughly simplistic. We have no expectation that a recovery of economic growth in the industrialized nations, in either the short or the long term, will alleviate these problems. Instead, we believe that all of us must confront the startling irony: these economic malaises, like a virus that has developed resistance or immunity to the cure, or like a pest that has produced a defence against the pesticide, have now become immune to the remedy of increased production growth. Ought we not at least to entertain the possibility that these dilemmas now stubbornly and successfully *resist* that proposed solution? Has their rigidity not in fact increased precisely in proportion to our efforts to solve them using the accepted economic instruments? Have not these economic dilemmas now become *structural*?

Consider, by way of beginning, several new and bewildering developments. At least six paradoxes have surfaced at the heart of the industrialized societies, including Canada – symptoms of a deeper malaise.

SIX PARADOXES

The Scarcity Paradox

Today's society, one of unprecedented wealth, experiences unprecedented scarcity. How is it that a society of enormous wealth also has growing scarcity? One would expect that increasing material prosperity would have decreased scarcity. However, even in an environment of increased economic growth and a rising standard of living, a new, generalized feeling of scarcity is permeating Western society. Though average incomes are substantially higher than they were 25 years ago, the belief in society that we do not have all that we need has become markedly more intense. Moreover, one can no longer ignore reports in the press stating that businesses, nonprofit organizations, and governments have had to slash essential expenditures and services. How is it that these reports appear much more frequently now than they did 25 years ago, when the average income was half of what it is today?

Perhaps the most blatant signal of escalating scarcity in the midst of unprecedented prosperity is the skyrocketing deficits of Western governments – including those in Ottawa and the provinces. Why do deficits soar seemingly out of control in the affluent nations, even under governments 'committed' to deficit reduction?

The Poverty Paradox

Poverty is rising sharply everywhere, even in the midst of affluent societies. Despite the development assistance and relief efforts undertaken over several decades by Canada and the other nations of the North, poverty and hunger have substantially *increased* in Africa and other parts of the world. Moreover, poverty is increasing at an alarming rate in wealthy societies. Again, one would expect that the creation of wealth would alleviate poverty. Yet consider first the pattern in the industrialized nations, beginning with Canada. Poverty increased from 14.2 per cent of the population in 1980 to 16 per cent in 1992, despite the substantial economic growth of the 1980s.[1] Likewise, though the 1992 United Nations *Human Development Report* ranked Canada the best place in the world to live, child poverty shot up from 14.5 per cent in 1989 to an astounding 18.3 per cent in 1991.[2] Currently, despite material prosperity, Canada has the second-highest level of child poverty in the Western world.[3] Poverty afflicts especially single-parent families, over half of which fall below Statistics Canada's poverty line.

In a similar vein, the US Federal Bureau of Statistics reports that in 1991 alone over two million more Americans found themselves in poverty than in 1990, bringing the total to 35.7 million, or to 14.2 per cent of the population. This is the highest figure in ten years. According to the Department of Housing and Urban Development, the number of people living in shelters grew by 155 per cent between 1984 and 1988, years that saw the longest peacetime period of sustained growth in the gross national product (GNP) in US history.[4] Even the lower of the wide-ranging estimates of the number of homeless suggests that more Americans are without housing than at any time since the Depression.[5] Between 1979 and 1989, the rate of child poverty increased by 21 per cent, while the GNP grew by more than 25 percent.[6] Further, poverty is encroaching on rural areas, despite astonishing levels of agricultural production.

The same paradox afflicts Europe. According to estimates, approximately 50 million people in the European Union live in relative poverty. Reliable estimates of the number of poor people in eastern Europe do not exist, but by all accounts the situation there is even more bleak.

The Care Paradox

In the midst of more wealth, we have fewer opportunities to practise care than before. Even as the standard of living rises, opportunities for carrying out 'sustenance' or 'preservation' are continually decreasing in number. Such activities include caring for people in hospitals and schools, for the elderly, for the emotionally distressed, for the condition of soil and water, and for the development of art and culture. Again, one would expect that more wealth would generate additional funds for such care activities and would free up the time that people need to undertake them. Instead, however, the reverse has happened: despite rising prosperity, opportunities for demonstrating care, both financially and personally, have decreased. How is this possible?

The Labour Paradox

Society's need for more labour is becoming critical even as unemployment rises. Despite the urgent need for additional labour, unemployment continually rises. Perhaps never in the recent past have the industrialized societies needed a greater input of labour. The tasks of rebuilding cities and towns, caring for people in need, and rehabilitating impaired ecosystems increasingly demand large amounts of labour. Why then is unemployment, instead of dropping, seeming to rise? And why does it appear not to drop even in periods of economic growth?

The Health Paradox

Even though our level of health care has markedly increased, our level of disease is rising. Despite stunning achievements and more extensive efforts in health care, the level of disease and illness in the industrialized nations is escalating. Not long ago, Canada's Laboratory Centre for Disease Control declared that science has failed in the battle against cancer, for example; despite the large sums spent, cancer mortality rates are rising, while 'the chances of an American getting cancer during his or her lifetime are one in three.'[7] Health care costs have reached a crisis. One would expect that a society boasting a rising standard of living would have raised rather than lowered its level of health. How is it then that the opposite appears to be happening?

The Time Paradox

Despite substantially more wealth, people have less and less free time. Citizens of the West, including Canadians, have less and less time for themselves and they find their daily activities more harried – again, despite greater affluence. In the early 1970s, experts predicted that, largely because of automation, the critical social problem of the 1980s and 1990s would be the possession of too much leisure time; in fact, however, despite much higher incomes, people now have far less time for non-work activities than they did in the 1970s. In *The Overworked American*, Juliet Schor concludes that in the past 20 years average working hours in the United States have gone up by the equivalent of one month per year.[8] Using data from Statistics Canada, Armine Yalnizyan has detected a parallel trend in Canada.[9]

CONCLUSION

The remarkable economic paradoxes described above reflect a deep malaise in the industrialized economies today. They are indications that the dilemmas of poverty, environmental degradation, and unemployment have acquired a new, perplexing element – their apparent resistance to, and even deterioration in the face of, efforts to solve them by means of industrial production growth. In part I, we sketch this development.

Part One
Why Economic Renewal?

1

Poverty, Environmental Degradation, and Unemployment

In the Introduction, we described several paradoxes that plague the industrialized societies. We suggested that these paradoxes are signs that the problems of poverty, environmental degradation, and unemployment have acquired a new, baffling element – they appear to be impervious to currently accepted solutions. In this chapter, we sketch this development. We trace the development of each problem over the last several decades from the vantage point of the success or failure of the attempted solutions, rooted largely in the much-vaunted remedy of a growth in industrial production. We also briefly consider the economic ramifications of the changing nature of international conflict after the collapse of the Iron Curtain. Together, these serve as the backdrop for the discussion of economic renewal in Canada and the other industrialized nations that occupies parts II and III of the book.

POVERTY

In the early 1950s, the first articles appeared about what we would later call 'development.' In 1949, US President Harry Truman sounded the political alarm for the world as a whole, when in 'Point 4' of his inaugural address he outlined the responsibility of the West with respect to poverty elsewhere in the world. Truman and others believed that the extensive transfer of capital – for example, in the form of loans with a term of 25 to 30 years – could remedy that poverty. Truman urged the West to earmark scarce production factors and capital towards the expansion of technological expertise in the Third World. He argued that the West had to set the economic machinery of the developing nations in motion by a 'Big Push,' starting with the creation of economic and social infrastructure.

Enthusiastic discussion and activity, particularly within the United Nations, then began over the planning and programming of the entire process. Canada was an eager and active participant, consolidating its efforts in 1950 through its participation in the Colombo Plan. Soon, however, those involved discovered that much more was at stake in the developing countries than an economic problem, much more even than the pre-eminent economic problem – scarcity. It appeared that vigorous cooperation would be needed if poverty was to be alleviated – cooperation among those in various scientific disciplines, politicians, and especially the poor. But clearly, by the early 1950s (or, actually, at the acceptance of the Charter of Human Rights in 1948), the industrialized West had opened up visions of a new period for the people of the developing countries. It spoke of *Rising Expectations* and of the *Prosperity of the World as a Mutual Responsibility.*[1]

Let us now step back and assess the success or failure of the 'Big Push' between 1950 and the present. At least five main themes emerge.

Rising Production, Falling Income

First, the period as a whole saw significant growth in production in the developing countries, averaging 3.3 per cent per capita of the population in the 1960s and 2.4 per cent in the 1970s. Production grew both in agriculture and in industry. After 1980, however, the income trend associated with production growth changed. For the developing countries as a whole, since 1980 income per capita has scarcely grown (0.1 per cent). In several regions, in spite of higher production, income per capita has actually dropped. The *World Development Report* (1992) of the World Bank reports that income fell each year between 1980 and 1990 by an average of 0.9 per cent in sub-Saharan Africa, 2.5 per cent in the Middle East and northern Africa, and 0.5 per cent in Latin America and the Caribbean.[2] This was a repercussion of the recession of the late 1970s, which for many Third World countries meant a substantial drop in their export prices – between 30 and 50 per cent.

The late 1980s and early 1990s have witnessed an increase in production in parts of the Third World, particularly in Asia, and to a lesser degree in Latin America. A comparable increase in Africa has not occurred. At the same time, a recovery of export prices does not appear to lie on the horizon.

Rising Numbers of Poor People

The World Bank estimates that the total number of poor people in the developing countries has increased without any interruption since 1950. By 1990, the poor in the Third World numbered 1.1 billion, up 0.1 billion from 1985.[3] This figure will probably continue to rise. 'Poverty' here means living at or below the 'poverty line,' generally defined by the criterion of the World Health Organization (WHO) – too poor to obtain a 'calorie-adequate diet.'

Subsisting below the poverty line has horrific consequences for children. UNICEF has estimated that 40,000 children each day, or about 17 million per year, die from lack of necessities or from exhaustion. Moreover, inadequate and inferior nutrition in the first year of life has serious consequences for the development of the brain. *Hunger 1992*, the report of the Bread for the World Institute on Hunger and Development, observes that 'one third of all children under the age of 5 in developing countries, or 177 million in all, are so poorly nourished that their development is permanently impaired.'[4] One can easily surmise the results. Africa has received the most media attention, particularly countries south of the Sahara. But sometimes even where production has increased significantly, the number of people living in absolute poverty has also grown dramatically. Perhaps the most well-known example is Brazil. Though it is the world's fourth-largest exporter of foodstuffs, it languishes under the world's sixth-highest malnutrition rate.[5] Despite notable production increases, 'today seven out of every ten Brazilians lack employment, fair pay and access to land to give them the diet defined as a minimum nutrition.'[6]

Widening Income Gaps

In most developing countries, production growth has not benefited all inhabitants: by and large, the rich have become richer and the poor have become poorer. The situation of the world as a whole – widening income differentials between countries – is now also becoming the situation within the bloc of developing nations itself. Important differentiations have cropped up within the bloc and have led to all sorts of categories, such as the 'newly industrializing nations' and the bloc of the world's poorest nations – those with extremely low income (averaging 1/50 of that of the G-7). Not only are incomes in the world's poorest countries exorbitantly low, but they continue to fall in absolute terms, and the number of poor people there rises.

The past forty years have also seen the beginning of a distinction between the relatively poor and the absolutely poor in the Third World. In certain countries, the income of one group of people has risen dramatically, and that of a second group much less noticeably, if at all. This situation has aroused anger and political tension. Over the last four decades, this gap has widened on a large scale in the developing nations, bringing with it political repression and human rights violations. Tragically, Asia, Africa, and Latin America have provided many examples.

In reality, only in a few countries has an improved economic situation led to higher income for all. Examples include Malaysia, Singapore, South Korea, and Taiwan. The nature of the industrial production in these and similar countries is striking. Women do the bulk of the factory work. Assembly industries, which are prevalent there, require long working days and offer low wages. If these industries are to continue in the Third World, they will do so using fewer and fewer workers, because automation and untenable working conditions will drive employees out of the workplace. The increase in production has generally been coupled with social disintegration, which becomes more acute as industries relocate.

Despite increased economic differentiation among developing countries, as a bloc they have worked together at international conferences. Thus speculation that a number of the newly industrializing nations would gradually add themselves to the Western group appears to have been premature.

Finally, income differentials across the world have widened sharply over the past three decades. According to the United Nations Development Program's *Human Development Report 1992*, 'in 1960 the richest 20% of the world's population had incomes 30 times greater than the poorest 20%. By 1990, the richest 20% were getting 60 times more.'[7] Similarly, the poorest 20 per cent receives only 0.2 per cent of the world's commercial bank lending, 1.3 per cent of its investment, 1 per cent of its trade, and 1.4 per cent of its income.[8] Duncan Cameron notes that in 1991, before taxes and social spending, Canada's richest 20 per cent received 48.9 per cent of total income, while the poorest 20 per cent garnered all of 0.9 per cent.[9] Indeed, a statement by the US Senate Committee on the Budget roughly typifies the situation around the world: 'At the start of the 1980s, a Chief Executive Officer made about 29 times as much as the average worker. Today that multiple is close to 100 times.'[10]

These figures help to explain a new, unexpected development – the increasing transformation of today's society into a 'dual' society. The 'dual' nature of our world society is reflected in the sudden, astonishing increase in the numbers of uprooted people streaming into the affluent nations. As John R. Evans observed recently in the *Toronto Star*, the G-7 leaders, at their summit meeting in the summer of 1993, identified the threat of uncontrolled migration as 'potentially more destabilizing than the proliferation of nuclear weapons or the prospect of terrorism.'[11] Uprooted poor are streaming into the United States from Mexico and further south and into the European Union from the south and the east. Lech Wałesa has eloquently described today's society as divided by a curtain made no longer of iron but now of silver. A silver curtain is not as thick as iron, and the wealthy nations find it impossible simply to lock their doors.[12]

Rising Debt

The rise in poverty is linked to the shocking burden of debt carried by many countries in the South. The burden has become so enormous that since 1982 the developing nations as a whole have paid more interest and principal to the wealthy countries and their banks than the total amount they received back from them in the form of investments, credits, and development assistance! According to the *Human Development Report* for 1992, 'the current debt-related net transfer from the developing to the industrialized countries stands at $50 billion a year.'[13] In other words, since 1982, the rising standard of living of the affluent nations has been subsidized by the developing countries.

The burden has devastated the economies of the poor nations. In 1990, their total external debt reached US$1.35 trillion. Since then, the overall figure has scarcely changed, though Africa's debt is still on the rise. But let us attempt to put the figure of $1.35 trillion into perspective. It means that every inhabitant of the North holds a claim of about US$1,110 on the countries of the South. In addition, each year he or she receives between US$150 and US$200 in interest payments from the South.[14] Conversely, the debt of the poorest developing countries stands at about US$81 billion, which means that each inhabitant living there owes approximately $176 to the wealthy nations, their banks, and their institutions. But the GNP in these countries stands at no more than $237 per capita per year! This leads to the astonishing conclusion that each citizen there must work nine months simply to pay off external debt.

And every child there, through no action of his or her own, is born into an astonishing debt obligation.

This paints a 'static' picture of Third World debt. But it is in the 'dynamics' of debt that the intractable, horrific reality of poverty in the Third World reveals itself. Four 'laws' govern the dynamics of debt today. They also make clear that the rising affluence of the wealthy nations is inextricably linked to the increasing impoverishment of the poor.

First, the poor nations must bear the full brunt of external shocks in the world economy, shocks over which they have no control. Only the rich countries have access to the creation of 'key' currencies, or currencies which are acceptable in the international exchange. In response to outside shocks, such as an imposition of higher export barriers or a raising of import prices (especially the price of oil!), the poor nations, simply to remain in position, thus have had to borrow from foreign banks money acceptable in international exchange.[15] To gauge the impact of these external shocks over the past decade, consider that, according to the *Human Development Report* for 1992, '20 of 24 industrial countries now are more protectionist than they were ten years ago ... [a reality that costs] the developing countries 10 times what they receive in foreign assistance.'[16] As an example, according to the North-South Institute, though Bangladesh is the largest recipient of Canadian foreign aid, Canada maintains substantial barriers on clothing imports from that country. If these barriers were lifted – Bangladeshi imports account for only 1 per cent of the clothing market in Canada – then the net gain to that nation would amount to almost triple the total amount of foreign aid that it receives from Canada.[17]

Second, debts increase despite significant effort to pay them off. This has occurred on a large scale. For example, between 1982 and 1988, the total debt of the Third World more than doubled, even though during that same period Third World nations paid US$830 billion to their creditors – an amount more than what they had owed in 1982! Similarly, in 1982, the low-income countries of Africa had an official debt of US$17 billion, against which they paid US$5 billion by 1986. Yet during that same period their debt doubled to US$34 billion.[18] Because of shockingly high rates of interest in the 1980s, the 'developing countries effectively paid an average real interest rate of 17% during the 1980s, compared with 4% by the industrial nations.'[19]

Third, debts rise because of the poor nations' attempts to pay off their debts. Irving Fischer's law ('the more people pay, the more they owe') has operated on a large and devastating scale.[20] The worldwide economic depression that began in 1979 reduced global demand for products from the Third World. Many poor nations, wanting to get out of the debt trap (especially because of rising interest rates), sought to increase their exports even more, because only that could bring in the 'key' currencies needed to pay off their debts. But in the declining world market, every increase in exports lowered prices. As a result, export revenues fell, and less money was available to pay off debts. Because of efforts to pay, the Third World's indebtedness grew.

Finally, the combined effect of these three laws has led to the fourth law – rising impoverishment while the Third World pays off debt. In the face of inability to pay escalating debts, creditors have required the poor nations to 'structurally adjust' their economies. The effects of 'Structural Adjustment Programs' have sometimes been catastrophic.[21] Frequently they entail lowering wages and decreasing by as much as one-third expenditures in so-called soft, non–export-related areas, such as health and education. Since 1990, the debt burden has required sub-Saharan African countries to reduce by one-third their expenditures on health and education.[22] Often, as in Brazil and the Philippines, structural adjustment programs require promotion of large-scale, export-oriented agriculture at the expense of local culture and appropriate-scale farming, which feeds the local population. Small farmers then become environmental refugees who have no place to live and no ability to feed their children.[23] The combination of lower wages, sharply decreased levels of health care and education, and loss of access to land has led to further grinding, relentless poverty.[24]

Indeed, the picture does not appear to be brightening. Before 1990, the World Bank calculated that 'debt servicing' by the African nations, or paying the interest and principal of their loans, would require annually about 5 per cent of their entire income. Calculate in an annual population increase of at least 3 per cent, and the scope of the problem becomes clear. If production grows by more than 8 per cent per year, then average income per capita in Africa will not decrease. But such a rate is out of the question. In the words of Robert McNamara in April 1990: 'The situation five years from now is likely to be worse, not better.' Infant mortality is again on the increase in Africa, and the continent faces 'the dismal prospect that [it] may enter the twenty-first century with a greater proportion of her population non-literate and unskilled than it did at the beginning of the 1960s.'[25]

Falling Expectations

None of this is to say that these realities have gone unnoticed. In fact, the expectations of those in the Third World had risen substantially with ratification of the Charter of Economic Rights and Duties of States (1989) and with the vision articulated in *Toward a Better International Economic Order* (1976), drafted at a special session of the United Nations. Based on these agreements, people sensed that political leaders would seek, however falteringly, to drive back world poverty. These documents sought to define the contours of an economy that would clarify the mutual responsibility of private institutions, national governments, and international bodies. They also sought to foster international recognition that the ideology of the 'invisible hand,' which has caused so much human suffering and injustice, has sent both us and our international economic structures down the wrong track.

During the last forty years, however, expectations in the Third World and among concerned people in the North fell considerably, for at least two reasons. First, in the developing countries, political liberation did not lead to the establishment of a new and unique relationship with the structure of the economy. It rapidly became clear that the pattern of economic relations, both within and between countries, was not easy to alter. In 1985, during a trip to the West, President Julius Nyerere of Tanzania stated that Western governments repeatedly tell the political leaders of Third World countries that they have made mistakes. Unquestionably, said Nyerere, they have. But, he added, 'Poverty and underdevelopment in Africa cannot be seen separately from the wealth and technological "headstart" present elsewhere. The existing pattern of the division of wealth in the world is a legacy which buckles over independent Africa. But it is not Africa's own doing. It is not insignificant that one-quarter of the world's population receives four-fifths of the world's income. Wealth creates more wealth, and poverty leads to more poverty, as a result of increased investment possibilities and one's power or powerlessness in relation to others.'

As for mistakes made by political leaders in the developing countries, we believe that in numerous situations, driven by self-aggrandizement, they have shown little or no interest in the poor of their countries.

Second, the development dialogue has produced a series of far-reaching ideas and well-formulated proposals.[26] The process in Canada has been fertile, producing such ground-breaking documents as the Pearson Commission Report (*Report of the Commission on International Development,*

1969), the Winegard Report (*For Whose Benefit?*, 1987), and CIDA'S report, *Sharing Our Future* (1988). In addition, five reviews of foreign aid policy between 1970 and 1994 offered urgently needed proposals for reform. None the less, lacking the political will to act constructively, Western governments, including Canada's, have never taken the vast majority of these suggestions seriously. Politicians have been able to move on effortlessly to other issues, partly because of lack of public interest in poverty. Sadly, in our assessment, misplaced optimism has weakened the resolve to implement fundamental reform, driven by the 'faith' that rising production and incomes will automatically 'trickle' down to all the people of the world, especially to those in the poor regions. Our understanding of economic processes and of the events of the past forty years does not support this view. In and of itself, rising production does not lead to just distribution: just distribution requires empowerment of the less well-endowed and an embrace of justice by the privileged.

In this context, if we consider poverty not just a human problem but also a matter of justice among nations, then the failure of the wealthy nations to live up to promises they made in 1968 is genuinely disturbing. In 1968, at the UN General Assembly, they committed themselves to earmarking 0.7 per cent of their GNP to financial assistance to the developing countries. In fact, however, only the Scandinavian countries and the Netherlands have lived up to this promise. While their contributions have exceeded 0.7 per cent, Canada, Britain, Japan, and the United States have fallen far short. Despite Canada's commitment, reiterated at the Earth Summit by then Prime Minister Brian Mulroney, it currently earmarks 0.44 per cent of its GNP for international aid, a figure that is projected to drop to 0.39 per cent in 1995.

To see this failure of the industrialized nations in perspective, consider that Maurice Strong, in an address entitled 'Beyond Rio: A New Role for Canada,' suggests that if the industrialized nations simply live up to their original commitment of 0.7 per cent, then they will have freed up enough funds to meet most of the objectives of the Earth Summit's *Agenda 21*, especially the primary goal of eradicating poverty.[27]

Poverty also poses an enormous challenge to non-governmental organizations (NGOs), including the churches – a challenge exacerbated by the failure of governments.

Conclusion

Faced with these baffling realities – declining income in the Third

World, despite growth in production; uninterrupted increase in the number of poor people in the developing countries since 1950; widening income gaps together with sudden, unexpected streams of uprooted people around the world; subsidization of the North by the South since 1982; the impossible debt burden of the developing countries; and falling expectations – ought we not to conclude that the form that the industrialized nations of the North have given to their responsibility to alleviate poverty is fundamentally defective? Indeed, it appears that the solutions used have either not helped or have dramatically worsened the problems. How else are we to explain the perplexing fact that even such distinguished international institutions as the International Monetary Fund (IMF) and the World Bank (launched at a conference at Bretton Woods estate in Washington, DC, in 1947) now find themselves engaged in substantial negative net transfers of money? The *Human Development Report* for 1992 states that 'between 1983 and 1987 net IMF transfers to developing countries turned from plus $7.6 billion to minus $7.9 billion' (with an annual average between 1986 and 1990 of $6.3 billion), while 'in 1991 new World Bank transfers were minus $1.7 billion.'[28] The report concluded: 'The Bretton Woods Institutions ... failed many developing countries at their time of greatest need.'[29]

Moreover, how else are we to understand the reality that *every day* an amount of money roughly equivalent to the total debt of the developing countries circulates uncontrollably in the world's 'pure' financial sphere – thirty to forty times more than that which circulates in the 'direct' sphere of buying and selling goods and services? These uncoordinated capital movements threaten the international monetary system itself, as we saw in 1992 when Britain and France were forced to defend their currencies by taking them out of the European Monetary Union.

Poverty and the failure of the 'Big Push' therefore present us with our first indication that today's economy must be fundamentally renewed. In spite of increased economic expertise and the vast expansion of technologies available for fighting Third World poverty, the baffling conclusion is that the main task is now larger than it was even ten years ago. We must locate and develop an answer, within the present economic order itself, to the seemingly intractable problem. Powers of death are reaping an increasingly grim, bitter harvest. The fact that *people* have created the present situation means that we must search much more seriously and diligently for the deeper-lying causes of poverty. And we must suggest what kind of renewal and reform are required if the industrialized nations, including Canada, are to pull back from a global economic system that has led all of us to the edge of an abyss.

THE ENVIRONMENT

Discussions about the environment began with *The Limits to Growth*, the first report of the Club of Rome, released in early 1972.[30] Since then, an enormous amount of material and data on environmental issues has been published.

The environmental degeneration flagged in *The Limits to Growth* has since become a reality in many areas of the world. At the same time, many people have begun to recognize that, because clean air, pure water, fertile soil, and sufficient quiet are essential to human life, environmental issues form a critical problem within economic life. More and more, we hear environmental realities described as 'new scarcities,' for example. In 1992, the United Nations Conference of Environment and Development (UNCED, or the Earth Summit), in Rio de Janeiro, Brazil, addressed environmental issues in a more far-reaching fashion than the Stockholm Conference had 20 years earlier. Recognizing that in many respects poverty is both a cause and an effect of environmental degradation, UNCED also linked the need to remediate environmental damage with the need to battle poverty.

These developments notwithstanding, over the last 20 years the environment has dramatically deteriorated. The assault on creation proceeds on a grand scale, despite legislation, individual efforts, the activities of NGOs, and certain substantial efforts within the business and scientific communities.

In chapter 6, we explore the extent to which *Agenda 21* (i.e., for the twenty-first century), the political agreement drafted at Rio, provides a genuine agenda for addressing the new economic and environmental realities.[31] At this stage, however, we supply a brief sketch of contemporary environmental realities.

The Ozone Layer

Depletion of the ozone layer forms perhaps the most serious environmental threat to the lives of people, animals, and plants. According to the World Resource Institute's *Environmental Almanac* for 1993, 'in the last decade, ozone depletion has overtaken smog and acid rain and has gone to the top of the list of human insults to Earth's atmosphere.'[32]

Twenty years ago, researchers recognized that the thinning of the ozone layer, largely through the emission of chlorofluorocarbons (CFCs) used in the production of a wide range of household and other products, would dramatically increase rates of skin cancer and cataracts in human beings. They now also know, thanks to studies from Australia, where the effects of ozone depletion are most advanced, that a thinner ozone shield allows damage to crops, harm to delicate food chains, and diminution in the durability of outdoor materials.[33]

Despite this knowledge, human beings have to date released some 18 million tonnes of CFCs into the atmosphere. According to Environment Canada's report *The State of Canada's Environment*, the world's CFC emissions have reached approximately 800,000 tonnes annually, while by 1987 annual consumption of CFCs exceeded 1 million tonnes.[34] The US National Aeronautics and Space Administration (NASA) reports that 'the earth's protective ozone concentration has decreased an average of about 20 percent over the past twenty years, largely as a result of interaction with CFC's.'[35] Skin cancers have increased dramatically over the past two decades. The United Nations Environment Program (UNEP) estimates that an expected 10 per cent ozone loss over a region covering much of Canada, the United States, and Europe will cause a 26 per cent increase in non-melanoma skin cancers and will generate 1.6 million new cataract cases.[36]

After years of opposition by industry, often in the form of minimizing of the dangers, 44 countries in 1987 signed the landmark Montreal Protocol on Substances That Deplete the Ozone Layer. Canada played a leading diplomatic role in the signing of the document. The signatories agreed to reduce CFC production by 50 per cent by the year 2000. Since then, many countries have vigorously sought to reduce the production of CFCs and have even independently stepped up their commitments. Canada and the United States have agreed to phase out production by 1996, while Germany will ban it after 1994. The need for these actions became much more acute when Mount Pinatubo erupted in the Philippines in 1991, spewing out an estimated 18 million tonnes of sulfate aerosol, another ozone-damaging substance.

From the start, however, experts have maintained that only an immediate reduction of CFC emissions by 90 to 95 per cent would salvage the ozone layer, because the 'lag effect' of ozone-damaging chemicals will mean ongoing destruction well into the twenty-first century.

Meanwhile, the signatories have revisited the Montreal Protocol and have formally agreed to ban CFC production worldwide by the year

2000. It remains to be seen, however, whether this injunction will be followed. Environment Canada has recently indicated that Canada 'will not be able to achieve even the more modest objectives set out in the 1987 Montreal Protocol, given current trends in emissions.'[37] To help ensure compliance in Third World countries, on 1 January 1991 the Multilateral Ozone Fund was established to help finance transfer of new technologies to developing countries; Canada will contribute $7 million.

Global Warming

The Intergovernmental Panel on Climate Change (IPCC), a group of scientists operating under UN auspices, estimates that a doubling of atmospheric concentrations of carbon dioxide from pre-industrial levels would increase average global annual surface temperatures by 1.5 to 4.5 degrees Celsius. Changes of this magnitude have never before occurred in human history.

These projections have generated considerable alarm. Many experts predict that global warming will raise sea levels and produce massive flooding and coastal destruction. They also anticipate that ecosystems will be unable to adapt, that tropical storms will become more frequent and severe, and that rainfall patterns will alter dramatically.

Meanwhile, at the Earth Summit, 153 nations signed the United Nations Framework Convention on Climate Change. However, 'the treaty does not set binding targets or require specific actions – largely at the insistence of the United States.'[38] Further, many critics believe that the treaty's stipulations are far too meagre: 'It calls for – but does not require – stabilizing emissions of greenhouse gases [such as carbon dioxide and CFCs] at 1990 levels in the industrialized countries by the end of the century.'[39] Though Canada has bound itself to this commitment, the Ontario Round Table on Environment and Economy estimates that the current 'impressive array of activities' will still not permit Canada to achieve this goal.[40] And because, according to an IPCC estimate, stabilization of concentrations of greenhouse gases at 1990 levels will require a 60 per cent reduction in emissions, the amount of such gases in the atmosphere will probably rise.

It is significant that 75 per cent of all emissions of carbon dioxide (CO_2), the principal greenhouse gas, originate in the industrialized nations. The United States is the world leader, both in total output and per capita. Annually it generates over 1 billion tonnes of carbon emissions, or 4.9 tonnes per person. Canada ranks second, at 4.4 tonnes per person per year. China, Germany, Japan, the former Soviet Union, and several other countries also contribute substantially.[41] What remains entirely unclear is how even a small decrease in CO_2 emissions can occur in practice. Levels of CO_2 emissions are closely linked to both energy consumption and transportation patterns, especially the use of automobiles and trucks. In Canada, the transportation sector, for example, contributes one-third of emissions, while electrical utilities and industry account for an additional 51 percent.[42]

A number of studies have documented the rising dependence on the car in the industrialized nations. Over the past 40 years, the number of cars on Canadian roads has increased eightfold, largely offsetting whatever gains have been made in controlling automobile pollution.[43] Each year Canadian automobiles spew out over 4 million tonnes of CO_2.[44] Further, studies have shown that the damage created by the car extends well beyond CO_2 emissions. It has been estimated that Ontario, for example, spends an additional $9 billion a year in 'social' costs (including policing, medical services, and others) associated with use of the car.[45] One-third of the area of Montreal is devoted to roads, bridges, parking, and other car-related uses.[46] When one considers, in addition to smog and local environmental threats, traffic accidents and fatalities, noise pollution, congestion and loss of time, land and space, then perhaps indeed 'one might reasonably argue that the car has diminished, rather than enhanced, our quality of life.'[47] The problems of traffic congestion are even more acute in highly dense urban centres in the Third World, where traffic fatalities are reported to be 20 times higher than in the industrialized world.[48]

Yet fanatic automobile lobbies have continually attempted to minimize such factors, preferring instead to glorify the car as a symbol of freedom and independence. In this context, it is significant that the concept of 'traffic calming' (for example, through diversion of cars) is beginning to take hold in Canada, with organizations promoting it in Vancouver, Edmonton, Toronto, Ottawa, and other cities.

Protecting the climate will cost huge sums (though not protecting it will cost much more) – money that the Third World does not have. The World Environment Fund, established at the end of 1990, is therefore important. Financed by contributions from the industrialized nations, it will serve to enhance Third World efforts to protect the world's climate. It thus runs parallel to the Multilateral Ozone Fund for protecting the ozone layer.

Acid Rain

Attention to air pollution over the past 20 years has focused largely on the problem of acid rain. Sulphur dioxide emissions, the principal cause of acid rain, have declined in the industrialized countries during that period. Indeed, the fight against acid rain in Canada is a relative success story. Thanks largely to public pressure, spearheaded by the Canadian Coalition on Acid Rain, Canada will have, over a ten-year period (1985–94), reduced emissions to 2.3 million tonnes annually, or to one-half of its 1980 level. Meanwhile, by its Clean Air Act of 1990, the United States signalled its intention to achieve the same 50 per cent reduction by the year 2000.

Yet it is clear that the issue remains a problem in various regions of Canada and around the world. Rain in eastern Canada has been found to be ten times more acidic than normal, causing an estimated $1 billion in damage annually in forestry, tourism, and agriculture.[49] Emissions have been not eliminated but merely reduced to an 'acceptable' average annual load of 20 kilograms per hectare.[50] Moreover, nitrogen oxide emissions form a second leading cause of acid rain in Canada, and 40 per cent of these comes from the transportation sector (automobiles alone account for 62 per cent of Quebec's nitrogen oxide emissions).[51] Almost one-half of Canada's land area has little capacity to buffer the effects of acid rain, while about 15 million hectares of forests has suffered decline and 'dieback,' largely because of acid rain.[52] Acid rain is also believed to cause or worsen respiratory problems, such as bronchitis and asthma, and a group of US medical researchers and physicians now regards it as the leading cause of lung cancer, after smoking.[53]

Meanwhile, the *Environmental Almanac* for 1993 reports that 'in many cases the use of very tall smokestacks has served simply to transport pollutants to another region downwind.'[54] One-half of eastern Canada's acid rain originates in the United States. Similarly, acid rain falling on Scandinavia has its primary source in England, the former Soviet Union, and eastern and western Europe.[55] The issues therefore have international dimensions. International conferences draft policy objectives, while the European Parliament entertains the possibility of a 'Delta Plan' against acid rain. It is about time: some experts believe that the damage caused to the continent's forests and lakes may be irreversible. Seventy-five per cent of Europe's forests are now experiencing damaging levels of sulphur deposits.[56] Estimates suggest that over half of the forests in the Netherlands are no longer thriving. Acid rain has damaged half of Germany's forests, while in eastern Europe the figure is even higher. Switzerland has begun to take steps against the ongoing destruction of forest areas in the Swiss Alps. In Scandinavia, air pollution originating elsewhere has poisoned fish in many lakes. Similarly, estimates suggest that 4,000 lakes in Sweden are 'biologically dead.' And acid rain harms not just soil and vegetation but also buildings, clothing, and health.

Biodiversity

The scope of the plunder of nature has also become evident in losses in biological diversity. Reports from the UNEP and the UN's Food and Agriculture Organization (FAO) speculate that 30 to 40 per cent of all known existing species may become extinct over the next 40 years. They surmise that this rapid loss of biological diversity will severely reduce earth's ability to supply species of medicinal and economic value, as well as genetic material that could help countries adapt to global warming.

The plunder of nature displays itself most spectacularly in the slash and burn of tropical forests and in the mass stripping of ecosystems in oceans and seas. These areas remain largely unprotected. The destruction of rain forests has received considerable media attention, largely because, though they occupy only 7 per cent of the world's land surface, they contain 50 per cent of its species. And so severe is overfishing that the Canadian government, in an unprecedented move, has banned all cod fishing indefinitely off the coast of Newfoundland and Labrador – an economic lifeline for these regions – in an effort to replenish stocks.

It was thus for good reason that the issue of biodiversity occupied a prominent place at the Earth Summit in Rio. Over 150 states signed the United Nations Convention on Biological Diversity, which has since come into effect. The Convention – which Canada promoted, both before and during the summit – calls for national strategies to protect biological diversity. Participants recognized that the biological diversity present in soils, for example, is essential to agriculture, to the integrity of forests and plains, and to human and animal health.

Yet implementation of the Convention remains uncertain. Canada's efforts have centred around setting aside as 'protected space' 12 per cent of the country by the year 2000. However, to meet this goal, Canada must reserve almost twice as much land in the next six years as it has in the past century.[57] Further, Environment Canada has pinpointed several major threats to biodiversity, including present methods of agriculture and forestry (which involve replacing mixed forests, which support diversity, with single-species tree stands), acid rain, toxic contaminants, and global warming.[58]

If future generations are to have the ability to provide for their needs, and if we are to prevent the ongoing destruction of species, then ought not the thinking and action of people living in the industrialized nations to change dramatically?

Toxic Chemical Waste

The scope of chemical contamination throughout the world appears to have exceeded earlier estimates by experts. Recent information detailing the amount of contamination and waste present in eastern Europe is startling. Soils and surface and ground waters around the world have increasingly become contaminated. Environment Canada estimates that more than 35,000 chemicals are used commercially in Canada – even as the health and environmental effects of the vast majority of these remain unknown.[59] In Canada, 8 million tonnes of hazardous waste are legally discharged into the environment every year.[60] Moreover, the Ontario Round Table on Environment and Economy has estimated that almost 80 per cent of the 4 million tonnes of hazardous waste produced in the province annually 'ends up in the environment untreated.'[61] Environment Canada speculates that as much toxic pollution enters Ontario from sewage systems as from direct discharge: 12,000 industries dump waste into sewage systems unable to treat toxic chemicals. And it estimates that there are 1,000 sites in Canada 'where contamination poses an existing or imminent threat to human health or the environment.'[62]

While some strides have been taken by chemical producers, the industry has shown an overall attitude of nonchalance, and it continues to create toxic waste with very little difficulty. Environment Canada observes that 'there are thousands of ... toxic chemicals entering the environment that have been neither monitored nor regulated.'[63] On a pro-rata basis, Canadian industries spend about one-third of their American counterparts on environmental protection.[64] In *The Politics of Pollution: Why Canadians Are Failing Their Environment*, Doug MacDonald chronicles what in his belief is the failure of Canada's regulatory system to curb the growth of toxic chemical production and discharge.[65]

The Union Carbide disaster in Bhopal, India, in 1984 brought the effects of the chemical industry into broad daylight, if only temporarily. It flushed out many questions. Spurred on by the event – in which approximately 3,500 people died and tens of thousands were disabled, many of them permanently – researchers have demonstrated that the Third World pays a proportionately higher price than the rest of the world, in the form of damage to health and the environment, for chemical production. According to the World Health Organization (WHO), each year pesticides in the Third World cause the deaths of approximately 20,000 people and illness for several hundred thousand. The developing countries are also increasingly becoming a dumping ground for hazardous substances banned in the West. In a macabre irony, the United States still produces and exports the banned substance DDT to the Third World.

The effects of toxic chemical pollution are also evident in agricultural practices in the North. Chemical fertilizer and pesticide run-off leaches into ground water and rivers to such an extent that it now seriously threatens the quality of drinking water. Approximately 40 per cent of all wells in Ontario, for example, contain chemical contaminants, the primary source of which is agriculture.

Agriculture

The degree to which issues in agriculture mirror the dynamics described in this chapter is striking. Agriculture has fared somewhat better in Canada than in the United States. Nevertheless, alongside unprecedented levels of production, it too is experiencing the three impasses outlined above – poverty (as evidenced especially in its crushing debt load), environmental degradation, and the debilitation of employment. And many farmers fear the potential effects of the recently completed Uruguay round of GATT talks.

The replacement of traditional farming practices with large-scale monocultural and petrochemically dependent agriculture has had a profound and well-documented impact. Many commentators, among them farmers, agree that loss of diversification has led to the severe disruption not only of delicate ecosystems but also of the rural communities that had to some degree been sustaining them.

Now-orthodox agricultural practices have led to soil and water contamination and to erosion on a vast scale. For example, according to the Winnipeg-based International Institute for Sustainable Development (echoing the report of the Senate Standing Committee on Agriculture, Forestry and Fisheries, *Soils at Risk*), Canadian farmers lose well over $1 billion a year from reduced production caused by erosion.[66] Every year, the Prairies lose 300 million tonnes of topsoil.[67] Rates of soil erosion in areas of the Maritimes have increased over five times since 1945, while Prince Edward Island has lost 50 per cent of its topsoil since 1900.[68] In southwestern Ontario, erosion has caused a 30 to 40 per cent loss in corn yields.[69] Other pressures on soils include salinization and urban expansion. Over one-half of Canada's prime farmland, for example, is located within a two-hour drive of Toronto.[70]

The unprecedented levels of production over the last 40 years have gone hand in hand with stunning increases in chemical inputs. Use of commerical fertilizer in Canada quadrupled between 1970 and 1985, while application of pesticides rose from 20 per cent of cultivated land to 50 per cent.[71] At the same time, the organic qualities of soils have declined (by between 30 and 50 per cent[72]), labour input has substantially decreased, and net farm income has steadily dropped, even as government subsidies have sharply increased. Greater use of pesticides and herbicides has also sparked concern over human health. Though such figures are difficult to establish with certainty, the National Research Council of the (US) National Academy of Sciences estimates that each year 20,000 additional cases of cancer occur in the United States because 'the average consumer is exposed to pesticide residues ... in nearly every food.'[73] Researchers have begun to link the pesticides present in food with North America's rising rates of breast cancer – rates that are four to five times higher in the West than in the poor countries – which make that disease the leading cause of death for women in Canada between the ages of 35 and 55.[74]

The Federal Farm Debt Review Board reported a 15 per cent increase in farm foreclosures from 1989 to 1990, while farm debt in Canada rose from $4.4 billion in 1970 to $21.2 billion in 1990.[75] Indeed, a debt crisis afflicts agriculture. Because of dependence on a single crop or livestock, large-scale, petrochemically dependent agriculture leaves a smaller and smaller margin for 'error' (such as too little or too much rainfall). Further, because the effectiveness of pesticides diminishes as insects develop defences against them, more chemical input is required, even as its price rises.[76] With increasingly little ability to rebound from or absorb 'error,' and with higher prices for inputs, farmers have had to borrow often large sums, particularly over the last two decades. Together these factors have made them even more vulnerable to wildly fluctuating prices and interest rates, resulting in the need to borrow even more. This situation in part accounts for grim statistics describing farm fore-closures.

These dynamics have also led to wholesale losses and dislocations in labour, driven in part by a bias against the assumed 'drudgery' of farm work. In certain respects, such dislocations may even reflect deliberate policy. In a 1969 report, the Canadian federal government released its vision for agriculture for the year 1990. Anticipating large, industrial-ized farms producing cheap raw material for food processors, it sug-gested that by 1990 two-thirds of existing farmers would be off the land.[77] Indeed, the last 40 years has witnessed what one commentator has called 'one of the most consequential migrations of history' – the movement, both forced and unforced, of millions of people from rural communities in Canada and the United States to the city.[78]

Clearly, large-scale agriculture has often meant even larger-scale dependence, and the slimmer the margins of error, the greater the scale of disaster.[79] However, Wendell Berry, Brewster Kneen, and others have shown that sustainable, diversified forms of agriculture and culture do exist, which preserve rural ecosystems and communities and remain relatively immune to the debilitating fluctuations of prices and interest rates. Increased crop rotation, the Integrated Pest Management Program, and the work of the Ontario Farm Environmental Coalition are signifi-cant. Reliable studies, based on actual farms and places, have demon-strated that, even on a large scale, farming practices that use little or no chemical fertilizers or pesticides can maintain, relatively speaking, both productivity and sustainability.[80]

Human Health

More and more today we read about the damage that chemical substances cause to human health. We have described several effects above. But inhabitants of islands in the Pacific Ocean, where France conducted unin-terrupted tests of nuclear weapons until 1992, provide further examples. The international community remained silent about these tests, though birth defects and chromosome damage have occurred there on a large scale. Even now, France has merely imposed an indefinite 'moratorium' on testing, pending further international security developments.

In Canada and the other industrialized nations, government regula-tions have lagged far behind the realities of the effects of chemical substances in places of work and on children. Canadian researchers have recently determined that ground-level ozone worsens asthma, which may help to explain a tripling of hospitalizations resulting from asthma over the past two decades.[81] And a recent UNEP report states: '1.2 billion city dwellers world-wide are exposed to excessive levels of sulfur dioxide. Nearly a third of the cities monitored within the Global Environment Monitoring System have levels of nitrogen dioxide that exceed the official guidelines of the World Health Organization and carbon monoxide levels in more than one half of the cities exceed WHO guidelines. Overall, only 20 percent of the world's 2.26 billion urban dwellers live in cities where air quality is acceptable. The health of many of the others is now being directly affected by high levels of airborne pollution.'[82] The *World Development Report* of the World Bank for 1992 states that only 2 per cent of sewage in Latin America is treated for sanitation.[83] Meanwhile, 1 billion people in the world live without safe water supplies and 1.7 billion without sanitation.[84]

Deforestation

Over the past 20 years, environmental problems have become critical in the Third World. In a number of regions, the poor must damage the environment in order to survive. The Brundtland Report on sustainable development, *Our Common Future* (1987), provided impetus for world-wide discussion of the fact that in many instances fighting poverty involves harming the environment, especially in the Third World.[85] The ongoing presence of poverty in the developing countries pre-empts a solution to the environmental problem there.

Deforestation and erosion form perhaps the most critical examples of ecological devastation in the Third World. They are, of course, closely linked. Poverty alone, however, does not create environmental deterioration. UN reports note that Asian electrical industries, for example, are the most polluting in the world. The concentration of carbon in the atmosphere over China and East Asia is higher than anywhere else.

While deforestation has received considerable attention of late, the extra interest has not brought an end to the destruction. In 1989, workers cut down or burned trees that covered the equivalent of 3.5 times the surface of Lake Ontario. Further, between 1979 and 1989, deforestation increased by 90 per cent. According to Norman Myers, Amazon forests will disappear in 28 years if the present pace continues. Vast destruction is also occurring in the Philippines, Sarawak, India, Thailand, Madagascar, the Ivory Coast, and Zaire.

Deforestation counts rapid erosion, floods, and climate changes among its effects. It also creates deserts, which Canada's International Institute for Sustainable Development reports are expanding around the world by 60,000 square kilometres a year, 'an area larger than Nova Scotia and Prince Edward Island together.'[86] The UNEP estimates that 35 per cent of the world's land surface is in various stages of desert-ification.[87] Reforestation programs offer meagre help, though they do help to reduce the amount of carbon dioxide in the atmosphere.

According to the *Environmental Almanac* for 1993, 'About 25 percent of the carbon dioxide released to the atmosphere comes from carbon released when forests are cleared. Thus, environmentalists worry that further deforestation will contribute to global warming, which in turn may lead to further extinction of many species as temperatures, habitats, and conditions change.'[88] Tropical rain forests provide a reservoir of genetic resources. Meanwhile, as noted above, the extinction of plants and animals proceeds at a pace of several species every day. Demand in the Northern Hemisphere for hard wood and cheap beef, coupled with the exorbitant debts of the Third World, significantly influences the current rate and scale of deforestation.

The Law of the Sea Convention

Though it has been difficult to ratify, by 1987 representatives of 159 countries had signed The Law of the Sea Convention, an agreement that gives proper due to the rights of Third World nations. Whether or not the convention will ever be enforced, however, remains unclear. The US Reagan administration put a damper over the entire affair, and as a result Canada and western Europe have hesitated to follow through. The agreement regulates, among other things, extraction of raw materi-als from the ocean floor. The US government, preferring to view the ocean floor as hunting grounds for private corporations, objected to that portion of the Convention. As a result, it effectively annulled the treaty.

Recently, however, the convention was ratified, and in 1994 it came into effect. Nevertheless, of the 60 nations that have ratified it, all but two (Iceland and Malta) are developing countries. Without the partic-ipation of a major developed country, it remains unclear whether it will be enforced. Canada could provide a powerful and urgently needed impetus by itself ratifying the document, into the development of which it put considerable effort. A number of Canadian experts have urged the federal government to do just that.[89] We are also gratified to read in the

'Red Book,' *Creating Opportunity: The Liberal Plan for Canada,* that 'A Liberal government will ... ratify the Law of the Sea Convention.'[90]

Energy Supply

Many of the problems identified above culminate in the issue of energy supply and its future. The world's people have consumed more energy since 1950 than in the entire history of the planet from its beginning until 1950. Since 1945, energy usage has risen about 5 per cent per year, which translates into a doubling of consumption every 14 years. A rising standard of living demands an increasing use of energy. North America is the largest culprit: together Canadians and Americans consume twice the energy that central Europeans do, and seven to eight times the energy that people living in the developing countries consume. Canada has the world's highest energy intensity per capita, while British Columbians consume 20 per cent more energy per capita than the rest of the country.[91] Meanwhile, in the words of the *Environmental Almanac* (1993), 'The combined production, distribution, and consumption of energy is the greatest single source of stress on the environment. It also poses threats to human health.'[92] Environment Canada observes that 'Canada obtains 75% of its primary energy from fossil fuels, the combustion of which leads to the three most important global air pollution problems – the warming of the earth's climate, acidic deposition and urban air pollution associated with ground-level ozone.'[93]

The primary sources of energy for household use in the poor countries are wood, manure, and agricultural scraps. While for people in the wealthy part of the world energy is largely a matter of price (for oil, gas and electricity), for those in the poor part of the world it is primarily a matter of mounting shortages.

Where then will the Third World find energy, if its inhabitants are to move to an adequate standard of living? Coal is plentiful there, but a coal-based economy harms the environment and leads to mountains of rubbish. Discussion of nuclear energy and its application has proceeded unabated, though no means have been found for safely disposing of nuclear waste. Meanwhile, the dumping of radioactive waste in oceans continues.

Since 1979, supplying energy by means of 'renewable' sources, such as the sun, wind, ocean, biogas, and water, has received more attention. These sources now account for approximately 20 per cent of both Canada's and the world's energy supply. Experts agree also that we can use energy much more efficiently than we do now.

Conclusion

Not long ago, the Canadian Institute for International Peace and Security predicted that in the future the succumbing of ecosystems will pose more of a threat to global security than national aggression: 'In the last few years ... people have begun to realize that long-term changes to the basic elements on which all life depends may prove to be as threatening – or even more threatening – than the nuclear war and military aggression against which we have been so assiduously defending ourselves.'[94] We shall not speculate as to which will form the more serious threat. Nevertheless, from the foregoing it is clear that an ongoing and unprecedented assault on ecosystems is occurring on a worldwide scale.

Some positive steps have been taken over the past 20 years. But how are we to assess the ability of current environmental efforts in Canada and around the world to reverse what US Vice-President Al Gore has rightly called 'the growing evidence of an ecological holocaust?'[95] How are we to understand their effectiveness in the light of Doug Mac-Donald's observation that 'the total quantity of pollution entering the Canadian environment each year has not been significantly reduced; in fact it may well have increased ... since the present regulatory system was established in the late 1960s'?[96] In her 1988 Christmas address, Queen Beatrix of the Netherlands stated: 'What we now face is the prospect of the annihilation of the earth not in a single blow but in a silent drama. The earth is slowly dying, and the unthinkable – the end of life itself – is still thinkable.' It seems clear that we must admit that our present-day solutions, despite the intensity of effort behind them, have not substantially slowed, much less reversed, the rapid rate of environmental destruction. Ought we not to conclude that, *in and of themselves*, current efforts do not and cannot address the root of the environmental malaise?

The entire complex of environmental problems – which appear to go hand in hand with current production methods and consumption patterns in the industrialized nations – thus offers the second indication that today's economy requires fundamental renewal. Evidently the current economic system is not in a position to safeguard the ecological stability that we require. That which is environmentally problematic is also economically problematic.

At the same time, a new economic agenda in industrialized nations such as Canada may not permit any solutions to today's threatening environmental malaise that impede efforts to alleviate poverty, both in the short and in the long term. And as we see below, such solutions must also not further debilitate the employment system.

THE EMPLOYMENT SYSTEM

Warnings sound not only from the biosphere but also from the 'sociosphere.' Unemployment in Canada hovers around 10 per cent. The figure stands in the United States at about 7.8 per cent, and in the European Union, at 10 per cent. Though reliable statistics for eastern Europe are not available, we may assume that overall they are even higher, and the Third World languishes under the realities of widespread joblessness, averaging between 30 and 40 per cent. To these figures we must add those people who, for whatever reason, rely on systems other than unemployment benefits. There are also large numbers who would like a job but whom the government cannot register as looking for work. The Organization for Economic Cooperation and Development (OECD), of which Canada is a member, estimates that in Canada, in addition to the 1.4 million officially unemployed, a further 1.4 million fall into the latter category.

In the industrialized nations, unemployment dropped slowly during the 1980s, only to rebound again at the beginning of the 1990s. The rise in employment during the 1980s ought not to delude us, however. Growth has consisted largely of part-time jobs, almost half of which, according to the Economic Council of Canada's report *Good Jobs, Bad Jobs*, are involuntarily part-time.[97] In addition, according to Judith Maxwell, former chair of the Economic Council of Canada, 34 per cent of total employment consists of non-standard jobs (part-time, short-term, or temporary).[98] Such work represents the fastest-growing segment of the labour force. And again and again today we read of massive lay-offs and job losses.

Indeed, the industrialized nations appear to be headed towards what already in 1958 Hannah Arendt labelled 'a society of labourers without labour.'[99] For do not today's production methods and the technological innovation that shapes them steadily eliminate employment? Between 1970 and 1990, the value of production in Canada increased by over 200 per cent, while labour input, in the form of total working hours, increased by only 50 per cent.[100] The connection between job losses and the structure of production remains concealed as long as economic growth remains strong, as it did during the 1970s. During the 1980s, however, the linkage came into broad daylight. For as we describe below, when the percentage of growth in productivity surpasses the percentage of growth in the GNP, as it did in the 1980s, then jobs are lost. Canadians therefore find themselves in a new dilemma – if they wish to maintain present employment levels, they must at all costs pursue uninterrupted growth in the GNP. Is this what they really want – and is the goal even possible?

The debate about employment has been advanced by research that shows that for most people the quality of work has markedly deteriorated, making work satisfaction a more acute issue. A Dutch economist, L.U. De Sitter, has attempted to explain this deterioration with a 'polarization hypothesis': 'This means that a direction develops within the labour market structure whereby both lower and higher qualified tasks increase in relative terms, but the tasks of the broad middle group decrease.'[101] Automation is also important: 'Automation either begins or strengthens a development whereby a division of labour creates a few qualitatively complex tasks but a relatively larger number of routine or menial tasks. Clear drops in the level of the meaning and quality of work occur in the larger *middle* group of qualified workers, such as qualified office employees (that is, trained and independent workers who are not part of management).'[102] In a similar vein, *Good Jobs, Bad Jobs* predicts that the 1990s will witness 'widening disparities in the quality of jobs and in the degree of economic security they provide for their workers.'[103]

Most discussions about labour do not consider whether a restructuring of industry can increase employment. They simply accept technological development as a given, even though it has considerable effect on both the quantity and the quality of work. The assumption appears to be that we may not tamper with technological development. But we recognize an element of truth in E.F. Schumacher's observation that 'modern technology has deprived people of the kinds of work which they have most enjoyed; creative, useful work requiring one's hands and brainpower. However, the work of mass production is fragmentary; and for the most part people take little pleasure in it.'[104]

Structural unemployment and the dwindling quality of work give us pause. For like other industrialized societies, Canada is rooted partly in the belief that work is one of the most important of all human activities. In the words of Hannah Arendt, 'The modern age has carried with it a theoretical glorification of labour and has resulted in a factual transformation of the whole of society into a labouring society.'[105] Is it not then bewildering that this same age has also engendered the 'prospect of a society of labourers without labour, that is, without the only activity left to them?'[106]

The authors belong to the generation that grew up during the massive unemployment and upheaval of the Depression. We were trained in the new economic science, which suggested that we could eliminate unemployment. While not supporting several premises of that economic science, we have sympathy for the principle of full employment. When everyone who wants to work can do so, then economic life has helped to give meaning to people's lives.

It is economists, none the less, who are largely responsible for narrowing the concept of work to paid work, which does of course perform many important functions. It helps people to begin and maintain relationships, to foster a sense of self-worth and self-esteem, and to assume a place in society and become involved in it. These benefits, however, seem to accrue much more to paid work than to unpaid. Often unpaid work offers little prestige. To make matters worse, even paid work does not always play a positive role in one's life. For many people, work means earning an income, and if they could stop working they would. Much work today appeals not to the whole person but to a piece of a person. This in itself has far-reaching consequences: the Canadian Conference of Catholic Bishops' *Ethical Reflections on the Economic Crisis* (1983) and Pastoral Message *Widespread Unemployment* (1993) frequently use the word 'suffering' in connection with work.

Faced with these realities – rising unemployment in the midst of economic growth, methods of production that appear inexorably to eliminate employment, and losses in the quality and prestige of work, especially of the unpaid sort – ought we not to conclude that the present-day solution to progressive debilitation of employment remains fundamentally defective? How else are we to explain the apparent imperviousness of unemployment to the remedy of production growth? How else are we to explain why unemployment appears to have become a structural feature of the industrialized economies? The human losses, together with an apparent inability to alleviate unemployment, thus form the third indication that the world's industrialized economies require fundamental renewal.

The need for a new approach to both paid and unpaid labour is therefore becoming urgent. Both the capitalism of today and the socialism of yesterday directly link labour to production. Neither acknowledges, in other words, the reality that labour may have meaning in and of itself. Instead, each locates the meaning of labour in the product of labour. But the people actually involved, as we noted above, often experience labour quite differently. Their experience suggests that labour may have an intrinsic as well as an extrinsic value.

Finally, if labour is becoming more and more scarce, then the relationship between labour and income deserves further consideration. For example, the Canada Pension Plan, the Unemployment Insurance Commission, and provincial health care plans, financed substantially by labour, may require revision. We return to this issue in step 5 of the final chapter. And when we discuss prevailing assumptions about labour, we also address (in chapters 5 and 8) the degree to which the present economic system will permit implementation of a renewed approach to labour.

AFTER THE COLD WAR

Changes in the nature of conflict among nations is relevant, though not central, to our deliberations. Such conflict is intimately related, however, to the appeal for the new economic agenda necessitated by the three economic impasses described above.

The most impressive event of the late 1980s was the fall of the Berlin Wall and the Iron Curtain. These events marked the end of a period of state terror and of large-scale, systematic human rights violations in central and eastern Europe. They exposed the deep-going failings of the state-planned economies. But most significant, they appeared to restore prospects of world peace, since the East/West confrontation had lost its meaning. The thorn had been removed that had led to an upward-moving arms spiral.

Without wanting to diminish the significance of that event, we want to grapple with the baffling fact that within one year the world's nations opted to resume travelling on the path of rising military insecurity. Consider, in addition to the Gulf War, the raging conflicts in Bosnia and in areas of the former East bloc. Shockingly, the enormous arms buildup in the Middle East shortly after the collapse of the Iron Curtain almost outpaced the earlier arms race engaged in by the East and West. While these tensions and buildups are primarily political matters, the Gulf War in particular has major economic ramifications.

The global 'return of military insecurity' after the end of the Cold War was not an accident. Its roots lay in the conduct not just of some people in the Arab world but also of some in the West. Economists have shown that access to the mineral resources of the world contains potential for conflict of which the scope is entirely unknown. Indeed, with the Gulf War a new element has surfaced: now it is primarily the affluent nations, not the poor ones, that find themselves compelled to acquire, with whatever degree of violence is required, guaranteed access to the world's oil-fields. Some of the rich countries – especially the United States – are enormous oil producers themselves, but their own production cannot match their much greater consumption. Though the United States ranks second in oil production in the world, 40 per cent of all of the oil it consumes is imported, which accounts for 60 per cent of the staggering US trade deficit.[107] The wealthy nations thus seek to live beyond the means provided within their own territorial boundaries. But their enormous economic power rests on lame feet. For without guaranteed access to economic resources from other parts of the world, their economies shake at their foundations. It is the giantism of the world's rich nations that increases the possibility of international conflict.

The gravity of the Gulf War lies also in the fact that it pre-empted the use of scarce resources for the sustaining of life in other parts of the world. This occurred on two sides. The countries of the North did not earmark the scarce resources freed up from the former arms buildup for peaceful ends, a task that the leader of the Soviet Union, Mikhail Gorbachev, had urged in a major address at the United Nations (in which he pinpointed reversal of the trend of worldwide pollution as one of the most important items requiring action). But the bitter reality for the South was that poor countries that do not produce oil were forced to help finance the Western arms buildup in the Gulf, because of the conflict's inevitable effect on the price of imported oil and because Western governments were careful not to raise taxes for this purpose. In other words, the poor countries had to help finance the startling global arms buildup, even though they themselves could not provide the basic necessities of life for their own people. The Economic Commission for Africa estimates that in 1990 the increase in African oil import costs caused by the Gulf crisis totalled $2.7 billion; India estimates that it lost $5.8 billion as a result of the crisis, and Pakistan, $2.1 billion.[108]

Such economic interactions occur often. The UN report *The Relationship between Disarmament and Development* systematically explores various connections between the increased production and sales of arms and the further entrenchment of world poverty.[109] Indeed, the two appear to be so mutually interactive that the reverse also holds: arms reductions, especially by the North, help to battle poverty. We see this even from the simple fact that arms escalation in the 1980s mushroomed the capital needs of governments in the North so much that it resulted in the substantial rise in interest rates mentioned above. This rise, of course, substantially aggravated the debt burden of the Third World.

In *Warfare and Welfare*, Nobel Prize–winning economist Jan Tinbergen has clearly shown that though international conflict directly affects economic processes, contemporary economists ignore it in their own investigations.[110]

DEFINING A NEW ECONOMIC AGENDA

Let us now return to our main theme. The persistent and deteriorating nature of the human and environmental tragedy described above has convinced us that today's industrialized economies, both in theory and in practice, must be fundamentally renewed. In the chapters that follow we argue that present-day economic theory and practice are incapable of adequately addressing poverty, environmental abuse, and unemployment. We claim that these impasses reveal critical structural flaws that are eroding the foundation of the social order of the industrialized nations, including Canada. These flaws become visible in the impact that poverty, environmental degeneration and the debilitation of employment have on people. Specifically, the economic impasses of our time harm relationships among people and with the creation. They violate justice, community, and peace.

But as we now embark on an investigation of what shape economic renewal ought to take, we need to consider yet another new and baffling economic reality: poverty, environmental abuse, and unemployment are no longer isolated entities. To a substantial degree, they may now form one problem. In the words of the Brundtland Report: 'These are not separate crises: an environmental crisis, a development crisis, an energy crisis. They are one.'[111] Though these words may sound ominous, they may give us a certain sense of hope. For if these dilemmas do indeed form one problem, then perhaps we can address them jointly from the perspective of a single solution, which current economic thinking and activity do not and cannot anticipate.

In what follows, we suggest that today's vexing economic problems, though often described in economic terms, are primarily crises of culture. They are partly sociopolitical and partly even religious. They will require more than technical solutions; they also require cultural solutions. In exploring economic renewal and the definition of a new economic agenda, we therefore examine the premises or assumptions about life that drive Western economic theory and practice. Indeed, the search for economic renewal must include an appeal to embrace different values that can ground an analysis whose ultimate aim is to encourage the development of a more humane and sustainable society.

But perhaps an objection arises: is it legitimate to explore values in today's context? Does not a plea to adopt new values trivialize the situation? Why would an embrace of different values automatically lead to greater humanity and sustainability?

Indeed, we believe that this assumption is questionable. Such an approach, which we may label a kind of 'voluntarism,' creates a false optimism: that societal structures simply dance to the tune of our desires and values. Ironically, a form of voluntarism lies at the heart of Western society; it is driven by the one-sided value that if everyone simply pursues economic self-interest, then we can automatically achieve 'the greatest happiness for the greatest number.'

We must therefore also address the exercise of economic power and control in society. The current structure of economic decision-making must play a significant role in our discussions and recommendations. Of course, certain new values – such as the recognition of the worth of the other person and of mutual responsibility – imply new power relationships. Likewise, when we work side by side with people whose needs remain unmet because of the manner in which society operates, then new perspectives may open up. Consequently, when we urge society to alleviate poverty and dependence, to implement a responsible environmental practice, and to open up the employment system so that it offers a place to everyone, we must do so from the vantage point of the disenfranchised and from the desire to voice the interests of those who now have no voice.

The plea to adopt different values must come from the vantage point of those who suffer under the present structures and the values that undergird them. But we must then also seek to transform exercise of economic control, and in the following chapters we offer concrete proposals on how such renewal might take place.

Part Two

Finding a Solution

2

Risky Calculations

In part I, we discussed poverty, the environmental malaise, and structural unemployment together. We now explore the possibility, alluded to at the end of that part, that they belong together. Is it possible that these three most significant economic impasses of our time have a common origin and that their simultaneous emergence is not an accident?

We saw above how paradoxical and unyielding these problems have become. They have acquired such an inner rigidity that many people have the feeling that something fundamental has gone wrong somewhere. We may feel as if we are passengers on a train that somewhere along the way went down the wrong track.

Or, perhaps more aptly, we may feel as if someone made a calculation that came out wrong. It is as if a calculation was drafted on behalf of today's society, and people have been working out the calculation in economic practice for years under the assumption that it would produce a favourable outcome. However, precisely now that the moment of truth has arrived, the calculation no longer appears to add up. To make matters worse, we seem to lack an opportunity to redo the calculation. For developments in the areas of poverty, environmental damage, and unemployment seem to happen at such break-neck speed and on such a global scale that they appear out of control. The burden of debt still hangs like a dark cloud over the poorest countries of our world, and our monetary system is so fundamentally unstable that even a minor shock causes it to shudder at its foundations. And social and military instability continues to increase.

Using this image of a calculation, let us propose a thesis. Perhaps the trio of economic impasses described above have their origin in a massive social calculation drafted by the discipline of economics and presented to society for implementation. Unfortunately, however, when put into economic practice, the calculation appears to lead to a perpetuation of poverty, the ruin of nature, and a rise in structural unemployment.

We test the validity of this thesis in this chapter. Our aim here is not to bring accusations against economic thinking as such. Rather, it is to focus on the links between economic theory and practice that occur in the industrialized societies. We explore the myriad connections linking economic theory and practice, of which people are often hardly aware. Is it not at least conceivable that enormous problems may arise, unintended, in economic practice because unsound theories and assumptions about life support the economic actions of people who, as far as they are concerned, are simply acting in good faith? Further, social orders often appear to have evoked and then entrenched precisely that type of economic thought that ensures their own survival. If this is the case today, then will not current economic thought obscure the reality of certain problems, and will it not serve several fixed economic interests rather than the interests of the entire population?

We therefore consider it crucial to explore the premises or assumptions that drive economic thought today. This ought to lead us back to the sources of the concrete problems described above. Moreover, it may create room for the entrance of other perspectives and approaches; and these will be sorely needed if we are to find different solutions than the ready prescriptions dispensed by currently accepted economic thought. In brief, we may describe the economic perspective defended in this book as the caring administration of what has been entrusted to us (the original meaning of the word 'economics'), an economics of care, or an economics of enough. With 'caring administration' as our starting-point, we find that an entirely different economic scenario emerges than the one provided by an economy whose trademark is the pursuit of more and more material prosperity, as measured in money. By now this trademark identifies not only today's economy but also Western society itself.

In this chapter, we first explore the 'calculation' that classical economists drafted and recommended to the society of their time. Then we consider the doctrine of contemporary neo-classical economists, and how it has perhaps obscured the reality of today's pressing local and global problems. Throughout we hope to nudge our thinking sufficiently towards a renewal of economic thought to inspect the three problems described above with somewhat better vision.

THE CALCULATION OF CLASSICAL ECONOMIC THOUGHT

Classical economic thought is two centuries old. It laid the groundwork for the calculation that most of society now endorses. A strain within it, utilitarianism, even adopted as its primary objective the making of a calculation for society as a whole – a 'felicific calculus.'

The felicific calculus was in essence very simple. Utilitarianism saw human happiness as being the result of adding up what was pleasurable and subtracting from that what was painful – adding 'utilities' and subtracting 'disutilities.' Working within this philosophical and ethical tradition, later classical economists identified the flow of all marketable goods as a stream of 'utilities' and the labour used to produce these goods, with all its drudgery, as a basic 'disutility.'

This 'happiness equation' had immense impact! It led immediately to the conclusion that human happiness is best served when a given input of labour produces as much output as possible. And millions in the West today regard this conclusion, which would equate a rise in the productivity of labour with an increase in happiness, as self-evident. Indeed, it more or less forms the heart of our economic order. But a number of premises or assumptions, each disputable and perhaps dangerous, lurk within it. One is that happiness is not something we receive but only something that we can achieve. Another is that the source of happiness lies directly in the amount of goods and services produced and sold in the market. Yet another is that because less human work means more leisure time, the less work we do the better off we are.

Utilitarianism is thus the first example of an economic thought intimately related to the fabric of the industrialized societies and to the directives by which they operate. More poignantly, however, it also obscures the reality of certain problems as they crop up. For according to it, less work, less employment, as long as that does not lead to a drop in production, is a benefit.

Another calculation made by classical economic thought has had a comparable influence. It suggests that we must follow the market wherever it leads, because the market will act as our guide to a better future for all. Naturally, for this to happen, we must permit the market to do its work with as little disruption and political interference as possible.

Adam Smith, the theorist who founded of this vision, spoke more humanely than many of his later followers. Faced with the abject poverty of his time, Smith inquired how the wealth of the nations, including that of the poor living in his own society, could be increased. Impressed by the scientific achievements of his day, especially by new production techniques, he identified two fundamental forces of production which he believed would lead all of society to increased prosperity: division of labour and accumulation of capital. For Smith, the well-spring of prosperity lay in the division or specialization of labour, which was made possible by the progress of industrial technology and by infusions of capital. But this well-spring could flow and have its beneficial effects only in and through the market. Because mass production requires large numbers of buyers, who by definition are anonymous, the optimal division of labour could occur only through unrestrained operation of market forces. Only through the 'expansion of the market' could entrepreneurs bring in enough capital to organize production processes and to supply enough machinery to create the necessary division of labour.

For Smith, the market was therefore the key to a better and more prosperous future. It was the institution by which human progress in technology and economics became visible. Not only that, but the market offered a way of measuring human progress (using prices and quantities) and of spreading progress around the globe. Indeed, for Smith the market played a role in all forms of human progress. It stimulated industriousness, culture, and the desire to save. Moreover, the market itself, led as if by an invisible hand, ensured the participation of the poor in the expanding wealth. Smith believed that its spontaneous operation led economic processes 'by an invisible hand to make nearly the same distribution of the necessaries of life, which would have been made, had the earth been divided into equal portions among all its inhabitants.'[1]

Is this a dead vision? Most definitely not! It has been transfused into the bloodstream of our Western culture. Consciously or unconsciously, we live it out in our society and propagate it around the world. We recognize in it the backdrop to many well-known premises undergirding economic practice. One such premise is that, as much as possible, the market must operate free of government interference. Indeed, the free working of the market lies close to the centre of Western society's self-definition: in the West it is not a government's place to tamper with the market, because this signifies a step away from a 'free society' and toward a 'totalitarian society.' A second premise is that, if a Third World country genuinely desires material prosperity, it must demonstrate its resolve by declaring that it is 'open for business' and that the free-market economy is welcome within its borders. It must then permit the money economy rapidly to replace the informal economy. And a third premise is that when we allow the market to do its sovereign work, then every poor person has the opportunity to get out of poverty.

All of these are deeply held assumptions – they inform the choices that people make, visions of life, and even the contents of one's faith. And in our time, after the breakdown of the planned economies in the former communist countries, they possess enough vitality to present themselves as untouchable truths.

In our assessment, however, these premises are not just questionable, they are misleading. They are misleading in their theoretical content, displaying the colours of the Enlightenment's naive belief in human progress and of a deist vision of society. They have as their undertone the mechanist worldview, which suggests that a good society must function like a machine whose operation is controlled by the laws of nature. And they show the texture of the more recent modern capitalism, whereby positive capital return automatically indicates the social desirability of a particular project.

More striking, however, these premises are misleading also in their demonstrable effects, which coincide with the economic predicaments described in part I. Classical economics sanctions the 'enlightened' self-interest of the individual as the cornerstone of all economic activity, and by definition it disqualifies any government intervention in the market. If, then, by listening to the voice of self-interest and obeying the dictates of the free market we benefit the poor just as if 'the earth had been divided into equal portions among all its inhabitants,' why concern ourselves with the division of the expanding prosperity? Why also concern ourselves with the state of the environment or with unemployment, if, as the classical approach assumes, the operation of the natural order permits humanity unrestricted cultivation of the earth, and if the operation of the market spontaneously increases employment? Indeed, armed with these assumptions about the world and about life, why trouble ourselves over a lopsided division of wealth, over destruction of the environment, or over the structural unemployment that eventually arises? The classical economic approach renders these concerns redundant and eases a guilty conscience in advance.

Modern economic science was launched with this calculation of market and self-interest. It went hand in glove with the new social order, or the 'new social fabric' (Carl Becker's term) that began at the same time. It was no accident that not until about 1850 did governments put into place the first serious corrections of production methods and of numerous other effects of the new economic order – such as the living conditions of the poor, the work hours of women and children, and the lack of any form of social assistance. For the science of economics had been silent about these forms of economic mismanagement. Even today, it approaches economic reality not primarily in terms of care, but in terms of the individual's pursuit of material prosperity.

Labour as a Calculation

Protest, critique, and the search for an alternative to this calculation came from another quarter: that of Karl Marx and Friedrich Engels. For them, pauperization, poverty, and exploitation were economic realities. Marx in particular attempted to uncover capitalism's laws of development. He formulated these laws in an economic theory that loads nearly every term with 'evil': a labourer is a 'wage-slave,' wages are equal to 'the reproduction value of the labour force,' and an enterprise's amount of profit is directly related to the 'degree of exploitation' involved. Marx and Engels argued that this was how capitalism deformed economic reality. Capitalism, they believed, turned people into objects, made work a form of enslavement, and alienated people not only from their social and natural surroundings but also from themselves. Can one then conceive of a greater contrast with the premises of classical economics?

Yet we must be cautious here. It was for good reason that John Hicks called Karl Marx 'the last of the classics.' Though Marx wholeheartedly rejected the theory that the sovereign operation of the market benefits all, and though he considered private property the root of all alienation, he was convinced that capitalism fulfills a 'historical mission' as a social form. He further believed that nothing is impossible for modern technology, that it is the use of tools that distinguishes humanity from the animal world (the human being is 'a tool-making animal'), and that the transition to a communist society is possible only on the basis of a full-fledged, automated production system. The poor will get their opportunity – but only in the context of belonging to the working class, which by definition is exploited; the environment will receive attention, certainly – but only in the context of the human manipulation of it. For according to Marx, no economic value can effectively come into being unless human labour is its source.

Therefore, it is incorrect to expect that Marxist economics and the economic order whose arrival it proclaims will ease poverty, environmental degradation, or structural unemployment. Neither in theory nor in practice has it emphasized, nor can it emphasize, the need to establish standards for technological development or to suspend economic expansion before all forces of production have been developed. Even less evident is a vision of humanity and the environment that would prevent them from being turned into objects of progress. We may say that in a certain sense, while Smith expected human well-being to spring from the sovereign activity of the market, Marx expected it to flow from the sovereign development of the forces of production, the fruits of which would come to the labour class by means of the class struggle. But for both theorists, it is labour that produces human well-being, which consists primarily in the abundance of produced material goods, thanks to an unfettered application of industrial technology.[2]

Neo-Classical Thought: Thought Lacking a Calculation?

Classical economic thinkers recommended 'calculations' about how a human society can become prosperous. Certain connections link these calculations to our daily thinking and action, to Western people in our day, connections we are hardly aware of. But do similar connections link modern, neo-classical economics with our daily thought and activity? And do they hinder or hamper us from finding genuine ways out of the crises of our time?

It is not as easy to answer this question as it is to describe the influence exercised by classical thought today. For since its inception in the nineteenth century, modern, neo-classical economic thought has attempted to protect itself from the reproach that it is making the 'value-laden' attempt to recommend a specific direction for society to take. In modern economic thought, we no longer find well-formulated calculations and recommendations about how we can become wealthy together. Responsibility for this issue has devolved to a separate discipline – 'welfare economics' – which now must handle this thorny question. Modern economics attempts merely to offer explanations, just as the natural sciences attempt merely to explain reality, as it searches for universally valid laws and undeniable facts that can be linked together in an objective and unbiased fashion. So it may seem that we cannot accuse modern economists of holding dangerous or unacceptable premises and biases, or of attempting to ease and allay the consciences of wealthy people and societies. For such concerns have no place in a 'value-free' science.

Or is neo-classical economic thought less innocent and 'value-free' than it appears?

Enter a Philosopher

The answer to this question arrives when we explore how the search for a 'value-free' economic science came about, and at what price. And the birthplace of this pursuit lies not with Adam Smith but with one of the most significant philosophers of the Enlightenment: Immanuel Kant. One cannot do justice to Kant in a brief discussion. Yet we must consider something of his thought, because it affects all of us closely.

Kant was a philosopher who wrestled for his entire life with the question of how reliable, objective knowledge is 'universally possible.' He sought knowledge that is not sullied or influenced by personal emotions or value judgments. He began by arguing that what we perceive of the world around us is ultimately nothing more than a 'chaos of sense impressions.' Then he wondered: can we obtain any genuine knowledge from out of this chaos?

At first glance Kant's answer appears modest. He stated that we can never actually know reality – the 'thing in itself.' But, he added, we can order our sense impressions, or give them an order. For example, we can distinguish between what comes first and what comes next in time, and between what differs spatially. We can also ascertain if one phenomenon causes another. In this manner Kant developed his doctrine of categories – principles by which one orders the chaos of sense impressions. Through the categories, knowledge arises that is not clouded by personal, subjective elements. In other words, through the categories genuine science is born.

What is striking is that a certain form of calculation or bias is not alien to Kant himself. He makes an attempt to return to the simplest elements (in this case, sense impressions) in order to rebuild the world from them in thought, as it were. Kant does not begin with a creation that has an order and has been entrusted to us by its Creator. Rather, he starts with a chaos above which broods the Spirit of Reason, as the beginning of all order. But what that Spirit orders is not yet a human society. It orders so that it can gather objective knowledge, knowledge that drives science.

Yet it would seem that this calculation is entirely different from one intended for society as a whole. Or is there a bridge between them?

Let us examine how the followers of Kant applied his ideas to economics during and after 1870. Like Kant, economists such as Carl Menger and Max Weber pursued 'genuine knowledge': in this case, genuine objective economic knowledge. But arriving at such knowledge is notably more difficult with economic phenomena than with physical. Under given circumstances, a stone always falls at the same speed. But if the price of butter rises, one consumer buys more while another buys less. Human behaviour is capricious and ignores static, natural laws. How then is it possible to arrive at science, at knowledge that is predictable and certain?

Faced with this question, the followers of Kant in economics took a similar tack as their master. If certainty does not lie within the given facts themselves, then one must construct a 'thought space' that makes certainty possible! The followers of Kant had to accomplish one feat to construct this thought space. They needed to work out of or expel from the study of economics all economic changes and developments that contain a seed of uncertainty. They needed to arrive at the point where all that remains for analysis and explanation is what is certain and what one can make positive statements about.

Here we stand at the cradle of what modern economics calls the 'data circle.' 'Data' are given factors or states of affairs that economics as such does not study, because it cannot make statements about their development with certainty. Human needs, motives, and desires belong to such data, which the neo-Kantian Strigl once called 'economic categories,' in the footsteps of Kant.[3] The economist establishes that someone wants butter, as well as the amount wanted, but he or she does not seek to understand this desire; it forms merely a given. Other such data (that is, given factors or 'starting-points' for economic explanation) include the nature and composition of the population, the state of technology at a particular moment, the existing social order, and nature. The question of how or why these factors develop is quickly referred to a practitioner of a different science. The task is to study only what functions within the given circle or domain of factors, which means that the economist is restricted to analysing only those entities that can be measured. In other words, the economist must confine himself or herself to analysing strictly the processes of the market mechanism. The issues therefore include the question of what prices change, whether the economy produces less or more, how much investment and economic growth will increase, and whether wages will go up or down. The economist can make so-called objective statements and formulate laws about these. As soon as the economist knows what people's needs are, or the maximum return that the entrepreneur seeks (or whatever else the entrepreneur seeks), what technological expertise is available, and so forth, he or she can begin to work. Based on these given factors, the economist can explain objectively and scientifically the operation of the market mechanism with 100 per cent accuracy, just as a natural scientist would. But the economist should never try to understand the data that surround him or her in the data circle, because such an attempt would damage or destroy the objectivity and certainty of the conclusions.

A DISTORTED WORLDVIEW

That was not an easy interlude. But it was necessary in order to discover how modern, neo-classical economic thought may have gone off track. Neo-classical economic thought has done almost everything it can to present itself as a positive (Hutchison, Friedman), neutral (Robbins), or objective science. To do so, economists have had to expel from their own field of investigation all forms of uncertainty about economic facts and relationships. They have had to 'work these away' to the data circle. But what a heavy price the science of economics has paid for this! Because of its drive to become 'value-free,' modern economics has lost value and credibility on at least four fronts.

Economic Needs

The first front is human economic needs. Economic science considers them capricious by nature, and it argues that any assessment of needs based on their own merits contains value judgments. Because it wants nothing to do with value judgments, economics merely accepts all needs as 'given,' as 'data'; it takes them as they present themselves to the market and asks no further questions. The same holds true for the desires and pursuits of entrepreneurs, unions, and governments. To economics as a positive science, economic needs and material desires form merely a point of departure, not a point of discussion.

Oddly enough, however, modern economics reserves for itself exclusive authority to render judgments about the efficiency of the means employed to meet these needs! Why is efficiency desirable? Does not a value judgment lie here? More important, do not human needs and choices themselves contain an economic aspect that economics as a science ought to investigate? If people can select means uneconomically, then can they not select ends or needs uneconomically? For example, is it not possible that satisfying the needs of one group or one society might jeopardize the possibility of meeting the needs of another group or society? In other words, if economics as a science can easily and uncritically accept as the starting-point for analysis every need presented to the market, then does it not legitimize needs in a certain sense? And because only those with buying power can register needs in the market, does it not legitimize the limitless needs of the rich in particular?

Our scepticism rises when we read in virtually every economic textbook that human needs are unlimited or infinite by nature. Consider whether this is true. If it were, then the whole earth, with all that it contains, would fall short of meeting the needs of just a few people. But surely this is a thoroughly Western, Faustian idea! We encounter here the thought-pattern undergirding what Tawney has called the 'acquisitive society,' – society that not only never has 'enough' but that also gives its own needs priority over others' needs.[4]

Therefore the first loss suffered because of economists' desire for a 'value-free' science is that economics no longer permits any form of 'needs criticism.' Even when such criticism is economically motivated, economists immediately refer it to ethics or political science.

Nature and the Environment

Acceptance of the neo-classical approach further means that nature and the environment become 'data.' Consequently, they fall outside the direct study and concern of economics. Economic analysis takes into account the state of the environment only after economic agents add environmental protection to their list of economic needs and register this by spending scarce means on it. The neo-classical defence of this practice is that changes in the natural environment belong to the field of biology, not economics. But does this apply even when the processes of production and consumption cause changes to flora, fauna, the atmosphere, and the soil? Does it also apply when such changes affect processes of production and consumption? The typical answer given by neo-classical theory is that any 'external effects' influencing production and consumption, such as changes in the environment, belong to the study of economics only if they cause a direct, objectively verifiable economic depreciation of scarce means – that is, of existing consumption or capital goods.

But here too we must speak of a real loss of the value and credibility of modern-day economics. Innumerable forms of production and consumption today cause tremendous long-term environmental destruction, which escapes the attention of us and our governments. To the extent that we do not register remediation of this damage on our list of economic needs, neo-classical economics does not consider it a direct, objectively verifiable economic loss. As a result, it does not enter the field of investigation of economics.

Yet are not human living space and human health just as legitimate economic 'objects' as a car or a dishwasher? In the modern economic framework they are not. If modern economics were to concede that these are indeed legitimate economic objects, then it would also have to concede that we can economically squander nature, health, and the environment. And then economic science could no longer consider all such environmental components as given – uninterrogated 'data' simply presented to the science of economics for analysis.

We see then that economics today recognizes only one kind of object for study – objects of use. Entities related to production or consumption receive an economic value (price) only when they are paid for and used. But the economic tasks of people and societies include more than simply producing and consuming; they also include care. Care is an authentic element of the oldest definitions of the Greek word *oikonomia*, or 'economy.' *Oikonomia* means the management (*nomos*), or care exercised by the economist, or steward (*oikonomos*,) for the household (*oikos*) and for that within it that is entrusted to him. With this definition of economics, it is no longer self-evident that human health, the environment, and natural resources poised for extraction fall outside the domain of economic objects. For economic objects now include objects of care. Economic life consists of more than producing and consuming; it also consists of sustaining and keeping.

Economic Accountability

There is a third consequence of relentlessly defining economics as a neutral science – elimination of the concept of economic accountability. If economics accepts all human needs, desires, and objectives as 'givens' whose rationality or origin it itself does not investigate, then what happens to the study of economic life and activity? Only the results of human actions expressed in prices and quantities remain for investigation. Only a kind of mechanism remains: a system of gears and sprockets of 'economic variables' from which people themselves, as living beings, disappear. Certainly, economic science includes individuals, organizations, and entrepreneurs in its explanations. It even identifies them by name. But they are not 'living' realities, but rather 'mummified' objects. They become more or less automatons, who in a given, presupposed manner simply react to the facts as they present themselves. Economic processes pass through them, as water runs through an eaves trough.

We may describe this situation in another way. When modern economics must explain something – such as an increase in unemployment, a slow-down of economic growth, or a rise in inflation – it never raises the question of who has caused the change or to whom it must be ascribed. Only the question of what the unemployment, slow growth, or inflation has set in motion is in order. Modern economics never views people, organizations, businesses, or unions as the actual cause of economic destruction. In the words of John Hicks: 'Causality is a matter of explanation; but when we explain, we do not necessarily praise or condemn.'[5] Praising and condemning have no place in a positive, neutral science.

But again we must state: how damaging it is, and what a loss for economics and society as a whole, that modern economic thought rejects any possibility of assigning responsibility for economic damages and ailments to their economic agents! The theory of economic policy refuses to consider the economic benefit or harm that people do to others; rather, it understands economic benefit and harm solely as effects of the good or bad functioning of the market mechanism itself. As a result, economic policy in practice usually attacks only the symptoms, not the real cause of economic misdoing. It remains entirely silent, for example, when a business jacks up prices or when a union demands too much. Without a means for economic accountability, modern economics in theory accepts everyone and everyone's desires uncritically and without question – within, of course, existing laws. But in so doing, it fully accommodates itself to our social order, whose deepest structural principle has become: 'Always obtain more for oneself.'

Human Labour

The fourth damaging effect of economists' drive for a 'positive' and 'value-free' science is that it has changed our society's view of labour. For classical economists, labour still functioned as the origin or source of all economic value: no value could come into existence other than that which came through human work. But modern economics pushes human labour from the centre to the periphery. Labour is now nothing more than one of several production factors. And like soil and capital, the two other important production factors, labour receives its economic value from the market. Without a market, work has no value.

This way of viewing work – as a paid production factor – is not only thoroughly familiar to us, it is in our blood, as it were. It therefore presents itself in ironclad logic, though it is the reigning economic system that constructs and defines that logic. Looked at from an economic perspective broader than that of scarcity measured in prices – such as that of caring administration – this approach to labour creates a serious reduction in at least two respects.

The first reduction lies in the valuation of labour. In the modern framework, labour is 'instrumental.' Work has economic value only to the extent to which it generates an income and functions as an instrument for producing goods and services, and only in so far as others have money to buy those goods and services. But does this tell the complete economic story about work? Where is the acknowledgment of what Max Weber called 'the intrinsic value of labour'? Where is the recognition that labour has value because it is human labour, irrespective of its accomplishments? Human well-being depends a great deal on the quality of work; indeed, the quality of work can make or break a person both bodily and spiritually. Therefore, economically speaking, we must see labour as more than a means of production. Because it is a human activity it is an 'economic object' in another sense: it is an object of care. What applies to the environment applies equally to human work – if we do not take care of it, if we treat it only instrumentally, then inevitably we have created a fundamental economic loss.

According to neo-classical economics, however, unless financial compensation has been arranged, a loss in the quality of work is not an economic loss. Without compensation, it is ungraspable; it is not sufficiently measurable and thus does not belong to the domain of economics. 'The quality of work' has significance only if people attempt to use their scarce resources to improve it. As long as they do not spend money on it, our economist has no interest in hearing about an economic necessity for preserving the intrinsic value of work. According to him or her, every such broader concern belongs to ethics, not economics.

A second reduction about labour occurs when one pushes labour from the centre to the periphery. It has to do with the kinds of work that people choose to do. According to modern economics, if one is to call something labour, it must be registered in a market – the labour market. 'Real' work is therefore paid work. If there is no price-tag, neo-classical economics cannot distinguish labour from leisure activities.

'Real' economic labour is therefore paid, paid at the price that management and labour have collectively agreed on.

But we must assert instead that perhaps the most important forms of labour are unpaid. Here too one's economic approach – whether one adopts the approach of scarcity measured in prices or of caring administration – is decisive. Many forms of human work involve the care and keeping of culture and the environment. They orient themselves primarily not to producing something for the market but to nurturing and helping people, social relationships, and ecosystems through time. From the perspective of care, work that produces products for the market we may call 'directly productive labour'; work that orients itself to the care and keeping of life through time we may call 'transductive labour.'

Transductive labour can be paid or unpaid. It includes such diverse activities as raising children, sustaining the environment, caring for and maintaining other people, performing in music and theatre, acquiring an education, and improving both urban and rural landscapes. The work of government departments and ministries also belongs to this sector. Part of what links all of these activities, whether paid or unpaid, is that they do not aim primarily to increase production, and they do not automatically bring their own financial return. They do not spontaneously earn their keep by way of the market. They can receive a financial reward, if people have so agreed ahead of time – something other than a wage (salary, honorarium, reimbursement for costs, for example) that people from elsewhere, such as the directly productive sector, must pay for, either voluntarily or through other means.

Current economic thinking tends to neglect the intrinsic economic value and significance of transductive labour. The reason is that transductive labour focuses on the care and 'maintenance' of the data in the 'data circle,' and the modern economist does not include such care and maintenance among his or her concerns. Instead, every emphasis lies on generating production streams to reduce the relative scarcity of goods and services registered by the market. The economist recognizes transductive labour only if it is paid or reimbursed. But the short-sightedness of this approach surfaces when we realize that the streams of goods and services generated by directly productive labour damage, with great ease, the 'stocks' and 'stores' of resources, ecosystems, human health and cultural heritage that still exist in today's world. When such damage to the 'data' occurs, transductive labour becomes more important instead of less so. Ought we not to learn a lesson from the so-called informal sector of the poor countries – namely, that it is unpaid transductive labour that keeps society afloat, and that the uniqueness and identity of a culture often lie here?

The distinction between productive and transductive labour sheds light on two of the economic paradoxes we encountered above: those of decreasing care and of decreasing labour in the midst of increasing material prosperity. Directly productive labour devotes itself to the market sector, where people make strenuous efforts to continuously increase productivity (remember the utilitarian calculation of classical economic thought). Rising productivity means that more products are made by the same number of workers or in the same number of work hours. In principle, the rising productivity of the production process makes possible higher incomes per capita each year, especially in the so-called advanced sectors of the economy. As productivity rises, the wage and salary levels of directly productive labour also rise. But modern society scarcely tolerates significant differentials in the increases of wages. As a result, each year we typically use potential wage increases in the advanced sectors as a standard for general, across-the-board increases in wages and salaries in our society.

However, in the care sectors of the economy, such as health, education, and welfare, which rely heavily on transductive labour, it is impossible to enforce the productivity increases possible in the advanced sectors of the economy. In fact, demanding them in hospitals, schools, and social work settings can destroy this relationship-centred work. As a result, every year the gap widens between what the care sectors must pay employees (because of the wage and salary standards of society) and what they are able to pay them (because of the slow rise in productivity in these sectors). This widening gap means that, as the prices of industrial products are able to remain the same or drop, because of increased efficiency, the costs and prices of services in the care sectors increase each year. Indeed, as we see more and more today, the costs of care become so high that they even become partially unpayable, certainly in terms of available public funds. This in turn drives labour out of the paid transductive sector, in proportion to the widening gap in productivity between the care and advanced sectors.

This phenomenon creates the labour paradox: in rapidly expanding economies, a continuous rise in productivity simultaneously increases care needs but decreases the volume of paid transductive labour available to meet those needs.

We return to this paradox in chapter 5. But we may identify a grim by-product of Western society's increasing inability to meet care needs.

As we saw with the poverty paradox, certain forms of poverty have reappeared and will reappear in the midst of affluent societies such as Canada. As is well known, what is relevant for the emergence of poverty is not just the amount of social assistance monies available but also the cost of living and the level of unemployment, both of which tend to rise as the costs of care rise. The 'fixed' living costs of every household are critical here. Higher costs for medical care and education directly affect the level of poverty of poor families. And the more that the costs of care increase in relation to the drop in price of industrial products, the more people on the poor side of society will become squeezed.

REVISITING POVERTY, THE ENVIRONMENT, AND UNEMPLOYMENT

We have now assembled enough elements and ingredients – such as the economic necessity of care and transductive labour, the distinction between needs registered and needs not registered by the market, the intrinsic value of labour and of the environment, and the necessity of economic accountability – for us to consider whether together they provide a better optic by which to view the origin of, and possibly the solution to, the trio of problems identified at the outset.

Throughout, it has become clear that neo-classical economics cannot help us with these dilemmas. Because it operates in terms of market, it misses entirely the large shards of poverty that the market is unable to register; because it approaches scarcity solely in terms of prices, it cannot assess the economic value of the ecological problem; and because it views labour solely as a paid production factor, it bypasses the problem of the quantity and quality of work. Neo-classical economics was not designed to help solve these problems. It seeks to understand and support only that which relates to production, consumption, income, and money in a market economy.

Therefore, by means of alternative economic concepts, we attempt below, however falteringly, to understand how these three pressing problems might have structurally embedded themselves in our world society. To begin, we offer Figure 1, a diagram that also employs elements from the thinking of economists such as Fred Hirsch and Herman Daly.[6]

In the top section, one can see that in today's economic order production factors are combined with production processes. The results then find their way into the consumption sector in the form of goods and services. The production process uses environmental factors, some of

Figure 1

Beginning 'Stocks'

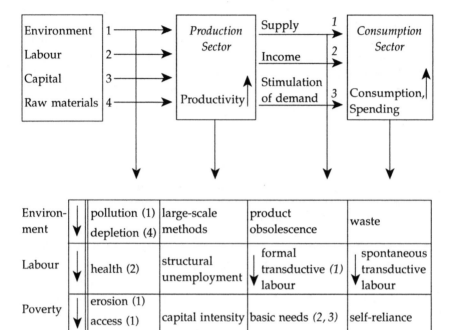

which are unpaid, and production must create income to make consumption possible. Continually increasing production assumes steady growth in the productivity of the production process. And on the consumption side, continually escalating production makes necessary influencing of demand through advertising in order to ensure a sufficient market for products.

On the bottom is a three-fold bar, whose headings describe, in terms of caring administration, the effects on people, culture, and the environment of the processes outlined on the top. It highlights the 'preservation' or 'stock' side of society, focusing on where increased production, consumption, and income change the nature and scope of care needs. The figure divides these effects into our trio of problems, with bars showing the effects on the environment, labour, and poverty.

The first bar, that of the environment, shows that progressively increasing production damages the quality of the natural environment. Rapidly increasing production and consumption extracts and depletes raw materials and energy from the environment and returns waste and pollution to it. Increased production and large-scale production methods (for example, aggressive, large-scale, and monocultural methods of working the land) intensify these harmful environmental effects as much as stimulating demand does (by, for example, shortening the life-expectancy of products and making disposable products). The combination of all of these effects led Herman Daly to call our societal production 'throughput.' Beginning stocks are 'rushed' through the streams of production and consumption at an ever higher tempo.

The second bar, that of labour, presents a similarly troublesome picture. Continual increase in productivity directly damages the stocks of spiritual and bodily health by overemphasizing the 'use' dimension of human work and underemphasizing its quality. But as we alluded to above, a continual increase in productivity also means that, in order to prevent loss of jobs, the overall rise in production must remain at least as great proportionally as the increase in productivity. In other words, as soon as the growth of the GNP falls below the average increase of productivity per labourer for the same year, a loss of jobs occurs. For example, if in a given year the GNP rises by 3 per cent and the average increase of productivity rises by 5 per cent, then a loss of jobs in the amount of 2 per cent occurs. In addition, as with the labour paradox, rising income made possible by production growth decreases the volume of paid transductive labour, because it becomes too expensive. Finally, increased income and consumption decrease the available time of consumers, as shown by Hirsch and others. People have less and less time and so have less time for spontaneous and voluntary transductive labour.

In short, paradoxically, an ever-increasing rise in the production of material goods in an affluent society creates continually more work at the level of caring for the environment and for other people, but opportunities for exercising this care continually decrease! This holds true for both paid and unpaid transductive labour. When combined with the negative effect that increased production efficiency may have on employment levels in the directly productive sector, the total effect on the supply of jobs may very well be negative.

The third bar shows something of the consequences of our continual production fury for the poor nations of the Third World. The top section suggests a positive result for the Third World: greater demand by the wealthy nations jacks up economic growth in the Third World, while the production supplied by 'our' transnational corporations there creates employment. But the bottom part shows several countervailing effects: rapid depletion of raw materials, which the poor countries can no longer use to meet their own needs; use of large-scale, inappropriate, and capital intensive technologies, which slows employment growth; occupation of land, which drives small farmers off their land, destroys communities, and, in general, decreases access to local resources; and income distribution and stimulation of demand through advertising that satisfy the luxury needs of some but, in so doing, reduce opportunities for others to subsist. Finally, rapidly emerging modernization in the Third World has the effect of attacking and debilitating the informal sector and its transductive labour.

Here too we draw the conclusion that an economic approach that takes as its starting-point the care needed to sustain people and the environment offers a much clearer explanation than current theories do for why the poor become poorer even in the midst of rapid modernization.

Finally, the reader may add a fourth bar showing the consequences of continual growth in production and consumption for peace and security throughout the world. Here the rising export of arms and the stronger demand for strategic resources and minerals lessen international security.

LOCATING A SOLUTION

Let us assume for a moment that our approach as a whole is correct and that we can explain the worsening and rigidification of poverty, environmental abuse, and employment problems in this manner. Does this approach help us to locate a solution?

We wrestle with this question in the remaining chapters. But let us consider an economy that places care needs first rather than last on its list of priorities and only then addresses the scope of production. In principle at least, such an economy, which places income and consumption levels at the disposal of care needs, will not worsen today's endemic problems. Such a reversal of priorities will reverse the direction of influence in the economy, so that the elements on the top half of the figure come under the influence of the care required in the bottom half. We may call such an economy a 'pre-care' economy. Our present economy is a 'post-care' economy; in it we engage in the highest possible consumption and production and only afterwards attempt to mitigate the mounting care needs with often extremely expensive forms of compensation.

Placing income and consumption levels at the disposal of care cuts to the core of the economics of enough. In it, a society or parts of a society instrumentally adopt income and employment levels (and with them, indirectly, production and consumption levels) in such a way that they serve the objectives of providing sufficient care for human subsistence needs, the quality of labour, the sustainability of agricultural and urban ecosystems, and improved development opportunities, especially for the poorest countries of the Third World. Because all these objectives identify fields of labour – both productive and transductive – implementing the economics of enough would also mean an end to the labour paradox. Where average incomes no longer rise, including those in the directly productive sector, there a path has been cleared for earmarking the resulting economic surplus towards the care activities required. And this will have the effect of no longer endangering the current volume of transductive labour.

3

Reclaiming People and Their Needs

Let us now take stock of the economic 'paradigm' operative in the industrialized societies today and then attempt to contribute to its renewal.

By and large, reports on the course of a nation's economic life render judgments solely on the basis of quantitative givens. Driving the assessment of these givens is the commonly held assumption that higher growth is good and higher growth than ever before is better. Conversely, a decline in growth implies that someone has made a mistake somewhere. And for a country such as Canada, which has boasted high growth figures for many years, lower growth is a sign of stagnation.

This premise appears to hold not just for the national economy but also for industry. Industry considers more return than the previous year good and less return bad; a poor return makes the stock market nervous. Industry almost always equates the lowering of costs with greater efficiency, and if a company can produce more with fewer employees, regardless of the consequences, then it is considered a success.

All of this reflects the unmitigated power of growth thinking. Again, we consider it better to grow by 3 per cent than 2.5 per cent, because the extra growth allows us to do more. A sprinkling of politicians may suggest where they would like to earmark the surplus, if they could, but we commonly assume that we shall spend the surplus on consumption. More consumption means more investment, which means more production. This is growth, and this is progress.

If the growth paradigm is indeed so deeply rooted in Western society, then some remarkable questions present themselves. First, have we derived any lessons from the events of the 1970s and 1980s? And second, what impact, if any, has the debate in the 1970s about economic renewal had? During that period, a series of compelling books and articles criticized the course of affairs in economic life, partly in reaction to the first oil crisis and the reports of the Club of Rome. Stirring appeals for economic renewal came worldwide from Binswanger, Daly, Eppler, Hirsch, Mishan, Schumacher, Scivorsky, and many others.

Let us consider these questions in the Canadian context in terms of our trio of economic problems. With respect to unemployment, the 1970s and 1980s demonstrated that robust growth does not always bring employment back up to previous levels. Ironically, in Canada, as in most of the West, unemployment in the 1980s did *not* drop dramatically, despite fervid economic growth. Similarly, as we saw in chapter 1, poverty in the Third World became structurally entrenched precisely during the 1970s and 1980s. Likewise, the increased production of those decades brought heavy pressure on the environment, which helped bring on the environmental crisis described in chapter 1.

Despite damage to ourselves, others, and the environment, today's paradigm appears to have emerged unscathed. Any potential lessons of the past two decades seem to have been ignored. Many people today tout expanded production as the solution to unemployment. Indeed, they often do so with a greater sense of urgency than ever before. Similarly, except for discussions under way in a few sectors of industry, the debate does not deal with the quality of work. In terms of poverty, attention to the poor gradually diminished during the 1970s and 1980s. To the extent that people in the affluent nations now devote attention to poverty in the Third World and within their own societies, they still work with the concepts of the 1970s. Finally, the increased production recommended for creating jobs will further damage the environment, certainly when unaccompanied by special measures and attention. The commonly accepted argument that we must 'earn' more through more production so that we can fund improvements to the environment puts the cart before the horse. Indeed, it brings to mind the plan suggested by the Ontario government during the 1960s to preserve the environment by encouraging Inco to build higher smokestacks, a plan that conformed with the thinking of the time.

In the 1980s, the debate about economic renewal appears to have become derailed. During the years 1980–3, the stagnation and partial economic decline begun in the late 1970s (partly because of the second oil crisis) demanded almost all of the attention in the industrialized nations, despite books and articles urging renewal and despite a good beginning in the public debate. In Canada, as in most industrialized countries, discussions about government deficits, unemployment, and social assistance appear to have accompanied debates about economic stagnation. Regrettably, the number of articles and books about renewing the economy tailed off sharply. Of our three major problems, the need to care for the environment occupied the most attention in the early 1980s, as, influenced by huge cost increases, industrial energy consumption dropped. And throughout the past two decades the industrialized nations have continued to use the GNP to measure growth and recession, both in absolute and in relative terms.

In the early 1980s, the authors of this book participated in a series of discussions with the chief executive officers of several Dutch transnational corporations, which took place on behalf of the Dutch Council of Churches and at the request of the World Council of Churches.[1] Despite the events of the 1970s, the business leaders held to an unshaken faith in the need to grow. Likewise, they consistently maintained that growth – meaning a growth in production – was a condition for solving the problems of poverty, the environment, and unemployment. We saw no trace of a sense of social responsibility that would compel the business community to set the course of economic life towards meeting basic human need. We discovered even less any trace of the recent debate about the social costs of production. Business leaders suggested that the government was responsible for any such costs but told us that by and large industry lobbied against current environmental regulations. They stated that industry usually considered them unnecessary and almost always too expensive.

Unfortunately, the CEOs do not form the exception. Politicians too display very little trace of the debate about renewal and the limits of growth. The old locomotive still stands on the rails, and many are busy trying to bring it up to speed. While many acknowledge in theory the presence of new scarcities – for example, of air, water and time – they do not show signs of this awareness in practice.

None of this, however, is to say that many people in the West do not hold lingering doubts about the current approach to economic realities or that we do not understand the desire to walk in the footprints of old and antiquated ways. Doubts have indeed surfaced. But how far do they reach? Will mere adjustments of economic policies and reformulations of the known pattern of economic ends and means be enough? Or must we perhaps dig deeper and reflect on an entirely different style of economic life?

RENEWING TODAY'S ECONOMIC PARADIGM

It is becoming clear that Canadians, displaying an 'intuitive leadership ... ahead of public opinion in other countries and well ahead of their own elected representatives,' are ready, with respect to the environment, to reflect on an entirely different style of economic life.[2] Surveys conducted quarterly by Environics Research and reproduced in the *Environmental Monitor*, reveal what one commentator has called 'nothing short of a *new economic paradigm* in the minds of Canadians.'[3] Assessing the survey data, Doug Miller writes:

Canadians are ready to confront false economies, where real costs are not reflected in the price for goods and services. They know these environmental costs must eventually be paid and a majority would prefer them paid up front through higher consumer prices, even in the midst of recession.

Canadians do not expect sustainability to come easily, or without significant personal sacrifice. A majority expect it will mean major changes in the way we live, including consuming less. As long as sacrifices are equitably distributed, they demonstrate a readiness to do their part.

These and other findings make it clear that Canadians are applying what they have learned from their environmental concerns to what they are now learning about the new economics. The result is a fundamentally new concept of economics in which Canadians see many opportunities and few risks related to aggressively pursuing sustainability. They are now looking for the leadership to move forward.[4]

Chapter 2 offers many arguments for reflecting on a new style of economic life. Economics has undergone a massive process of reduction in an effort to become 'objective' and 'value-free.' As a beginning, ought not then the discipline of economics, as a partner in society's overall economic orientation, to catch up to the alteration in attitudes identified above and entertain the possibility of a 'paradigm shift'? Perhaps economists should return to deliberating about the foundations of society. They would not find themselves alone in such a self-examination. A number of researchers from a wide range of disciplines have embarked on paradigm discussions, in which they define 'paradigm' as the intellectual model used to interpret reality and to discover practical ways of action. As a beginning, economists might ask themselves precisely what they want to pursue. For since the Second World War, they have asked primarily only how things happen.

Consider, for a moment, the irony of this request. Traditionally economics has maintained that its object is people and their needs. Have not its practitioners, then, in an effort to make themselves irreproachable as scientists, perhaps gradually strayed from the basic premise of economic science itself?

With the post-war 'mixed economy' and construction of the welfare state, economists themselves attempted to soften several of the harsh sides of their own neo-classical framework. By means of the mixed economy, they have attempted to correct a number of the harrowing consequences of their own paradigm. In some respects, this development has been positive. The mixed economy encouraged economists to include the theory of political economy as a new subdiscipline, and welfare economics made clear that growth and accumulation are not always the best means for combating unemployment. It likewise led economists to re-examine the idea of 'consumer sovereignty.' It generated their interest in the distribution of wealth, and it contributed to the insight that redistribution could help to increase national prosperity. With it too arose a willingness by economists to develop a budget mechanism alongside the market mechanism, to recognize the need to provide adequate care for people, and to integrate this concept into policy.

Given the economic and cultural crises of our time, however, these modifications have not gone far enough. For in its foundations, as we saw in chapter 2, economic theory remains incapable of addressing the root causes of poverty, environmental damage, unemployment, and the diminishing quality of work. It also has not and cannot adequately address the effects of economic activities on social and political structures. It cannot reverse the abandonment of the role of intermediary institutions and the resulting concentration of power, nor can it speak to the cleavage between people and nature. Finally, it is unable to deal with the dominance of the market as the means for solving problems in the local and world economies.

Our ultimate goal then is a renewed ethic of economic responsibility within Western society. We argue below for such an ethic, which seeks to pursue the interests of others rather than self-interest. As authors, we turn to the scriptural injunction to love God and our neighbour to help define the heart of this ethic. Love of God and neighbour stands at the centre of the Gospel. It seeks justice and knows the difference between justice and injustice. Thus we seek, from out of this perspective, to help define a new and renewed notion of economic responsibility and a renewed economic paradigm.

Economic science has always said that it wants to orient itself to people and their needs. Given the observations above, has not economic science perhaps left its moorings? And ought not Western culture as a whole, including Canadian society, to adopt this maxim as a starting-point for its renewed economic paradigm?

But if we accept this classical economic maxim, then clearly we cannot mean only some people and their needs, even if they number several hundred million. Nor can we mean satisfying the material desires of several hundred million people without paying attention to the basic subsistence needs of future generations. We must, in other words, locate an economic paradigm that incorporates the needs of *all*. Western society cannot accept the reductionist battering by economic science of its original premise. Instead, we must frame a renewed interpretation of the old economic maxim, rooted in the desire to meet the needs of the other.

Becoming oriented to the other leads us to define three dimensions of a renewed paradigm. We propose that industrialized societies such as Canada accept as their first priorities meeting the needs of the poor; reordering the priorities of the rich; and giving due weight to the needs of future generations.

The Poor

As we saw in chapter 2, concern for the poor is not just a matter of ethics. It is an issue which, when economics has been defined rigorously and consistently, belongs to economics itself. Because any approach is unreliable if it does not take seriously its own premise (in this case, care for people and their needs), the needs of the poor properly belong to economic life itself, even if the market cannot register them. Today's predilection for satisfying the material desires of people living in the Northern Hemisphere thus creates a dilemma, at the point where meeting basic subsistence needs crosses over into the satisfying of material desires. And increasingly in our time meeting material 'needs' pre-empts the possibility of meeting the genuine economic needs of others. Those of us who live in the North must now confront this dilemma head on. We must also focus on the economic differentials dividing groups of people, including those who are entitled to financial assistance. Naturally, all of this also has significant ramifications for economics itself.

The industrialized societies must therefore focus on the poor – those

who live at or below poverty levels, who live in life-and-death circumstances, such as the children who die each day because of starvation
and exhaustion. Those who live in affluent countries often find it difficult to imagine the oppressive grip of poverty. But again as authors we
turn to the injunction to love God and our neighbour. In the Gospels,
Jesus announces freedom to the poor. The German theologian Jürgen
Moltmann writes about the poor:

The poverty meant [by Matthew and Luke] extends from economic, social and
physical poverty to psychological, moral and religious poverty. The poor are all
those who have to endure acts of violence and injustice without being able to
defend themselves. The poor are all who have to exist physically and spiritually
on the fringe of death, who have nothing to live for and to whom life has
nothing to offer. The poor are all who are at the mercy of others, and who live
with empty and open hands. Poverty therefore means both dependency and
openness. We ought not to confine 'poverty' in religious terms to the general
dependence on God. But it cannot be interpreted in a merely economic or
physical sense either. It is an expression which describes the enslavement and
dehumanization of man in more than one dimension. The opposite of the poor
in the Old Testament is the man of violence who oppresses the poor, forces
them into poverty and enriches himself at their expense.[5]

Information from the world of the poor shows that many are becoming conscious of their situation. They have always known that they are
poor. But now they also know why they are so. Historically, the perpetuation of poverty has been associated partly with efforts to convince the
poor that they will gain a future reward for their poverty, and it is
striking that gradually this too is now changing. If earlier the poor
simply accepted their fate, now they are realizing that their situation is
the result of an economic and social order adopted by others, an order
that can be changed. They have set submission and passivity aside. In
some regions, a Marxist vision feeds this process; in other regions, a
Christian vision has brought inspiration and renewal.

In a number of Latin American countries, the poor have found that
the biblical stories contain their story. They have recognized themselves
in them and are actively drawing out the consequences. This in turn
confronts the rich in the developed countries with a challenge, which
in our view we in the North have not yet sufficiently taken up. Proposals framed by the World Council of Churches, the Catholic church, and
other ecclesiastical bodies to take steps towards solidarity with the poor

have thus far remained unanswered. Our impression remains that the theological community of the developed countries still does not allow sufficient room for the Christian faith experiences of people from other cultures and races. And until this happens, theology in the developed world will not be genuinely ecumenical.

Nevertheless, the ecumenical movement has strongly encouraged the passion for public justice. For many Christians, public justice is linked inextricably with a biblical understanding of God. The South African theologian Allan Boesak writes: 'God is glorified when the hungry are fed, the naked clothed, and the homeless are given shelter. God is glorified when children are able to grow into healthy adults and God is glorified when we use our resources to fight poverty, seek justice and love peace.'[6]

This concept of public justice helps to give some content to the renewed paradigm and economic practice that reclamation of the classical maxim demands. It suggests that in a society those needs must take priority that make life possible and preserve it. It calls the rich to adopt the principle of restitution: return of possessions to their original owners. This is how we understand the story of the Year of Jubilee (Deutoronomy 15, Leviticus 25) and its re-emphasis throughout the whole of the scriptures. With this story, the fulfilment of which Jesus adopts as his mandate on earth (Luke 4: 18–21), God announces freedom from want and from fear to *all*.

The Rich

We are aware that all of this has serious consequences for those who live in Canada and the West. It means, for example, transforming current understandings of 'charity' and 'stewardship.' We must not merely ask what to do with our money, but we must raise the prior, more fundamental question: 'How did I receive the money I have?' The church itself must provide an answer, because behind it lies the reality that wealth has accumulated in the hands of a few, while many people on earth die of hunger and misery. The church must further entertain the prospect of change. In the light of those people whose very lives are immediately threatened, the church must set aside the fear and trembling that shackle us in the face of the unknown, and it must begin to change. For immediate threat to life is a daily reality for hundreds of millions of people living in the developing countries.

People will show more inclination for change when they realize that present economic certainties are illusory. To the degree that information about poverty and chronic environmental abuse improves, to the degree that people perceive how fragile their own economic course is and how disadvantageous are the growing economic differentials within their own societies, perhaps they will understand the illusions lurking behind our present economic activity.

How then do we renew the economy so that a broader perspective can emerge within it for the poor? We must begin by defending the insights that we have already acquired and that often come under attack during difficult economic times. We must, for example, fight the fallacy that economic growth by definition can cure poverty or unemployment. We must argue the case that though increased military expenditures do expand production and employment, such growth may be economically fatal. We must promote the notion that when we simply apply the market mechanism, invariably the unused productive forces orient themselves to those with the highest incomes. In sum, we must urge Western society to renew its outmoded economic approach so that alleviating poverty becomes paramount.

But then we must define basic economic principles. And in today's context, broad ethical principles, such as alleviating suffering, meeting need, combating injustice, and reducing violence, suggest such a basic economic principle. The West must accept a minimal provision for our own basic needs (as well as for the basic needs of all), in conjunction with establishing a level of maximum consumption.

Let us consider, by way of two examples, the principle of accepting minimal rather than excessive provision for our needs in the West. Today much of our consumption of food is excessive and harmful. A UN report shows that in the rich nations the indirect consumption of grain in the form of meat and dairy products has reached such a scale that it causes human health to suffer. Along with this, in all of the rich countries 'prosperity diseases' – food-related and other conditions caused by a rising standard of living – have driven up the costs of health care. These same countries also squander food. To make matters worse, as Wendell Berry and Brewster Kneen have noted, the astonishingly high food production of the affluent nations increasingly threatens the sustainability of the land and of agricultural communities. In *What Are People For?*, Berry writes that this productivity 'is based on the ruin both of the producers and the source of production.'[7] The food industry itself shows little interest in these problems, and most people have yet to resist the advertising that hawks the 'new' products put out by the food industry. The majority of industrial food producers use 'more and more' rather than 'enough' as their catch-phrase, even though we live in an age of over-consumption and pay a heavy price for it.

But let us assume for a moment, as Berry's title implies, that people are not made for production, but production for people. We must then implement the concept of 'enough' in the food sector. For the sake of the poor, the sustainability of agricultural ecosystems and communities, the stabilizing of our health and our health care costs, we must pursue a sufficient, or minimal level of provision for our food needs.

A second example comes from the field of energy. An avalanche of literature has shown that our sloppy handling and over-consumption of energy form a serious threat to the environment and to the ability of future generations to provide for their own needs. Though the 'experts' consider the development of alternative energy sources impossible, and not just because of the costs, recently work has surged on developing such sources. Despite little investment and incentive, the number of solar, wind, and other forms of power applications rises each year. For example, Toronto's renowned Hugh McMillan Rehabilitation Centre, an 86-bed hospital for children with disabilities, is installing a 100-kilowatt solar-cell photovoltaic array, 25 per cent of which is already in operation.[8] In the United States, the municipal utility in Sacramento, California, operates a massive, one-megawatt photovoltaic array adjacent to the Rando Seco nuclear power plant, the first stage of a 100-megawatt solar-cell power plant.[9] And according to a recent *Washington Times* report, a technical breakthrough in solar-cell design makes possible a cost projection for the production of electricity with solar cells that matches the cost of electricity produced by fossil fuels.[10] Similarly, wind-generated power is 'surprisingly competitive.'[11] A new windfarm in southwestern Alberta, near Pincher Creek, will soon supply almost 10 megawatts of power to the provincial grid.[12] These and other examples of the inroads made by new alternatives teach us that public priorities can help put the economic engine on track.

Conversely, developing a standard of maximum consumption is desirable for several reasons. First, pressing for a strategy to ensure that basic subsistence needs are met has no credibility if the affluent countries themselves do not constrain their own material desires. We cannot use the excuse that human needs are infinite. Such an assumption, regardless of its validity or lack of validity, cannot direct responsible action. Second, by accepting such a standard, perhaps in the form of an income policy, industrialized societies will slow the continual increase of real incomes, which we drive up in order to 'keep up with the Joneses.' This change will ease performance pressures in the money economy as well as creating avenues by which to improve the quality of life. Third, accepting this type of standard creates room for implementing the principle of restitution mentioned earlier. Fourth, discussing the desirability of such a standard can highlight the negative aspects of our 'consumption society.'

Finally, as we discuss opting for a standard of maximum consumption, we must consider the relative poverty present in our own regions. In addition to the indications of burgeoning poverty within Canada and the industrialized nations cited in part I, consider that in Canada 131 foodbanks have opened since 1990, bringing the total number to over 2,000 – more than any single grocery or restaurant chain, including McDonald's. None the less, it is more and more difficult to meet the demand for emergency food. Further, in Toronto, 45 per cent of users are children.[13] In the United States in 1991, there was a 26 per cent increase over the previous year in requests for emergency food assistance in major cities, only 17 per cent of which were met.[14] Clearly we must realign the forces of production in such a way that, in addition to providing basic subsistence to the poor in the Third World, we meet the needs of these people in the North. For theirs too rank among genuine economic needs, not desires for material luxury.

Future Generations

Creating a strategy for establishing a standard of maximum consumption flushes out a weighty question. What form of economic growth is legitimate, and for whom do we need it? This introduces the third dimension of a renewed economic paradigm. Is a type of economic growth possible that does not harm the subsistence possibilities of future generations? Current economic activity gives virtually no account to future generations. At present, as we noted above, production and consumption have effects on future generations that the market does not register but which nevertheless are very real. Though environmental contamination occurs gradually, it is conceivable that in a few decades it will become irreversible. Aspects of the extraction and depletion of resources, both of raw materials and of the nonrenewable sources of material prosperity, also figure in here. Those who as yet have no voice – the unborn – will discover the harmful consequences of our ways of producing and consuming.

Environment Canada has touched on this dimension of a renewed economic paradigm. Its report *The State of Canada's Environment* contains this passage:

Humanity is thus caught on the horns of a dilemma: make the significant life-style changes implied in reducing fossil fuel use in order to slow down the rate of climate warming; or maintain current lifestyles and be forced to adapt to the economic and environmental consequences of a warmer climate. This is one of the most difficult dilemmas of our time because it challenges the very basis of our prosperity: the use of cheap fossil fuels. ... As evidence continues to mount that present patterns of energy consumption are environmentally unsustainable, future energy directions must begin to address more difficult trade-offs, *including the impacts of current energy choices on future generations.* As yet, all nations still do not have a solution to reconciling the burgeoning demand for energy with the need to maintain a viable global ecosystem.[15]

We submit that in a renewed economic paradigm no form of economic growth is legitimate that violates the limits of sustainability, either for the poor today or for future generations. We violate these limits when we use raw materials for products of dubious value. We also violate them when, for the sake of consumption in lucrative markets, we convert agricultural and horticultural production to create non-food products.

SELF-INTEREST OR THE INTEREST OF OTHERS?

The plea for Canadian and Western society to adopt a renewed economic paradigm and practice assumes that change is possible. It also assumes that, to a certain extent, the economy can be 'guided,' because clearly without some form of guidance one cannot expect the market mechanism to deliver a good outcome. Without other measures, the operation of the market will not promote the 'humanization' of society and culture. Who then will guide the economy, and on behalf of whom? We return to this delicate issue at a later point. But clearly democracies need new sources of inspiration on this point. And in view of the dominance that the economy enjoys over social life, renewing the economic paradigm means that we must develop a new public ethos and regauge today's values. People must also describe, by means of a broad public educational effort, what is involved and what is at stake.

In our opinion, a renewed economic paradigm must proceed from the assumption that people need to advance the interests of others. They must be willing to think inclusively. They must choose to be led by considerations other than self-interest, a principle that belongs inextricably to the thought-patterns of the industrialized societies. Many economists and others still accept the thesis that self-interest plays a positive role in motivating people to reach higher achievements. But unless they can see an immediate and direct benefit from a certain action, we question whether people act strictly out of self-interest in every respect. In view of what neo-classical theory calls the 'external effects' (for example, the influence of production on the environment) of everyday economic activity over the intermediate and long term, we seriously question whether self-interest can be beneficial. Instead, it often seems to serve a negative purpose, for we display much selfishness, both individually and collectively. There is also much that we overlook and much that we do not know. The principle that the individual's pursuit of material prosperity generates 'social harmony' creates false hope. Jeremy Bentham's utilitarian maxim – that when we pursue 'the greatest happiness for the greatest number' we will automatically create social harmony – has never been borne out.

Herman Daly proposes an alternative that we believe ought to inform Canadian and Western society's renewed paradigm. He suggests that we pursue 'sufficient per capita product for the greatest number over time.'[16] He uses here a term which, as we have seen, can prove reliable – 'sufficient' or 'enough.'

In contrast to 'growth,' 'enough' defines a relationship with the poor. It likewise has significance for the question posed above in this chapter – where is the boundary dividing desire for material luxury from the legitimate economic needs of people today and in the future? It helps to define in today's context the basic economic principles of minimal provision for our needs and a standard of maximum consumption. But economics alone cannot locate the boundary, for it is also a political and cultural issue. We must discuss it as broadly as possible, and we must articulate an answer in policy. The context for this discussion is that rising production now appears to create new scarcities – for example, of air, water, and time. These scarcities arise because rising production in the over-developed West violates the limits of sustainability, which in our view we have already violated.

In summary, by promoting a new or renewed economic paradigm, we have sought to strip off the restrictions that have shackled economists over the last several decades. We emphatically reject the reductionist paradigm; instead, we urge society as a whole, including economists, to reclaim the original focus of economics, namely, people and their needs. We do so because of the need to opt for all people, and in all respects. We advocate bringing the dynamic elements of real life back into society's economic paradigm. When this is done, real life supplies us with two new sources of information, flowing out of the lives of vast numbers of people living in poverty locally and in the Third World and of those belonging to future generations. These souces and who they represent cry out for an altered practice rooted in a renewed paradigm.

4

Renewing the Economic Order

Let us consider where we have alighted along the way. In chapter 1 we described the main economic problems facing the world today: mounting poverty, the deterioration of the environment, and the loss of meaningful employment. In chapter 2 we suggested that these problems have a common origin. In one way or another, they all have to do with 'calculations' implemented by the industrialized societies, and they no longer seem to add up. We saw that the science of economics actively participated in drafting these calculations, including those designed to solve poverty, environmental abuse, and unemployment. Economic theorists formulated them in terms of market, profit, labour, and growth, but never in terms of the caring administration of what has been entrusted to us, which is the meaning of the word 'economics.' That brought us in chapter 3 to explore whether we might locate another economic paradigm, and we arrived at an economics that takes as its first priority the real needs of people – an economics of the poor and of the carrying capacity of our environment to sustain future generations. We have alighted, in other words, on an economy of pre-care, which places care needs first on its list of priorities and only then addresses the scope of production.

Having said all of this, however, we find that the problems described in chapter 1 recoil upon us like a boomerang. For how, inspired by a different approach, can we alter our full-fledged, post-care economic and political practice? This practice is pervaded by calculations built on money, growth, and the market, and only after pursuit of these do we seek to alleviate the mounting care needs. The question itself may sound presumptuous, because people may not even desire a different economic practice. A certain need has developed in Western society to make calculations as we do now and not differently. For not only have these calculations become embedded within our habits and traditions, but they have also been incorporated into the societal order or structure in which all of us live and move and have our being.

Consider, for example, a Canadian business that attempts to convert on its own to providing more care for the environment, improving the quality of work, and retaining as many jobs as possible. It will quickly price itself out of the market and go bankrupt, simply because of the costs involved. When seeking to redress poverty, environmental damage, and unemployment one brushes up against nothing less than the powerful influence of a societal order whose signature is progress measured in money. And societal orders or structures do not easily surrender to change, as we see again during eastern Europe's difficult transition from a planned to a market economy.

LESSONS FROM THE PRESENT

In this light, how realistic is it to expect that today's economic order can actually change? The answer hinges on our assessment of major recent events, especially the fall of the Iron Curtain and the subsequent Gulf Crisis. Specifically, do we see these occurrences as a sign of the strength or of the weakness of the economic and political systems of the West? If we see in them simply signs of strength, then we may have no reason or desire to pursue or expect change.

A current interpretation of what caused the Gulf War is that the entire international community had a compelling interest in denouncing as quickly as possible any violation of human rights and of the principle of self-determination (in this case, of Kuwait). If we accept this view, then we interpret the Gulf War as a sign of the strength of the international community and of the leading states, such as the United States and Canada, in particular. A parallel interpretation of the fall of the Berlin Wall understands it as an indicator of the inner strength of Western society and of its economic system. After all, our system lives on, but the planned economy collapsed before our very eyes! From this vantage point, both incidents affirm the order of society as we know it, while in the European context they serve as the success formula by which to chart the continent's future after its economic unification.

In chapter 1, however, we proposed a somewhat different interpretation of the Gulf War. The fact that the rich nations had to intervene so quickly in a place where, at most, a regional conflict had flared up, had a great deal to do with an economic practice that has no recourse but to walk in dangerously oversized shoes. The United States ranks second among the world's largest oil producers, but its own production cannot match its own much larger consumption, which ranks first in the world. Therefore, when the assurance of ongoing massive energy imports flagged, the United States reacted as if it had been stung. Did not US President George Bush, echoing a statement he made at the beginning of the confrontation, declare at the Republican National Convention in 1992 that the 'decision to confront Saddam Hussein ... assured the continued flow of oil to the rest of the world'?[1] The Gulf War then also reveals a fundamental weakness inherent in a superstate's enormous exercise of power: those who wish to walk in oversized shoes become treacherously dependent on others. When Saddam Hussein invaded Kuwait, he touched the Achilles' heel not only of a political superpower but also of a highly dependent Western economic order.

The fall of the Iron Curtain also requires a second reading. We can begin by raising the sober question of why the centrally planned economy failed. It starts, in other words, when we examine the planned economy as an economic system as such, not just as a weapon for securing the regime of a political/military dictatorship bent on terror and destruction.

There are many reasons why the centrally planned economy was a failure, and all played a role in the collapse of the economic systems behind the Iron Curtain. Some have to do with how a single central plan operated in a complex economy that had long lines of command: it struggled through an enormous scale of bureaucracy and corruption, glaring inefficiency in production, and the wasting of soil and energy through the most unrealistic forms of price-setting. But there are also other significant factors. In a planned economy, any plan, however decentrally applied and expertly implemented, is plagued with built-in limitations, which, when ignored, avenge themselves on the outcome of the plan. Specifically, each plan must have a quantitative slant – that is, be formulated solely in terms of prices and quantities. Further, each plan, whether geared to the short or the long term, approaches the future only as if it is an extension of the present. Its goals and projections can rely solely on what is known about the present and its state of affairs.

It was then no accident that the planned economies behind the Iron Curtain were fraught with crippling flaws. These problems reared their heads precisely when external shocks struck that fell outside the plan's frame of reference – such as when the quality of the environment and of society as a whole entered the picture. For no plan could entertain non-quantitative realities. And as one might expect, figures that described the present state of affairs often formed highly unreliable descriptions of the future.

Such assessments of the structural flaws of the planned economy are highly useful, because they reveal basic structural flaws that afflict not only the operation of a central plan. Indeed, the institution of the market is plagued with similar problems! Like the planned economy, the market economy requires an exclusively quantitative slant. As we saw in chapter 2, in a pure market economy nothing has value unless it has a price. Although one might assume that culture, nature, and human health have substantial value, from the vantage point of the market they have none: the market uses and employs them at no cost (at least as long as the government does not intervene). Further, the market cannot identify needs unless people lay money on the table, and without a financial return it cannot organize production to create supply. Of course, one cannot level this criticism at the institution of the market itself, which cannot be other than merely a world of money, prices, and quantities. Yet the quantitative limitations of the market become extremely dangerous when a society no longer acknowledges them, as occurs when it uses the market as its ultimate compass. This is an example of what Daly and Cobb have called the 'failure of misplaced concreteness.'[2]

Similarly, the very flaw that threatened the sustainability of life under the centrally planned economy plagues the market economy. Nobel Prize–winning economist Jan Tinbergen has shown that in a market economy long-term scarcities have no influence on today's prices. Because markets have a 'time horizon' of no longer than eight to ten years, in a certain sense they are blind to the future.

This sober diagnosis shows that we cannot interpret the collapse of the planned economies simply as a sign of the strength of what presents itself as the sole remaining alternative: the pure or mixed market economy. On the contrary, their collapse also indicates the weakness of that economy. For sooner or later, the defects that tripped up the planned economies will cause the market economy to stumble, and for precisely the same reasons. Both types of economies are oblivious to that which is non-material and non-quantitative, and both remain oblivious to the future.

In truth, the collapse of the Iron Curtain demonstrates that everlasting life has not been granted to any economic order, whether it be the planned or the market economy.

Of course, recognizing that the present economic system may well fail over time, particularly if we are unwilling to alter it, does not in and of itself create a better or more sustainable alternative. It does, however, throw into a different light those convictions that hold that change is neither possible nor desirable. For now it would at least seem meaningful to consider what steps Western society must take and what obstacles it must overcome to become a society of caring administration, which permits the development of a sustainable economy. In this chapter, we identify three areas where society must reorient itself: prioritizing and limiting its own ends; organizing and applying the means to meet these ends; and distributing and using economic power and influence to support these shifts.

Economic Ends

To implement an economics of care, the industrialized societies must alter their approach to economic ends. Specifically, they must redefine the consumption goals served by the production system. Building on our paradigm discussion in chapter 3, we may distinguish three types of economic ends: material luxury desires, which are either harmful or frivolous; needs that are real and significant but not essential to the preservation of life; and basic subsistence needs. From this rough and necessarily somewhat arbitrary categorization we may 'tease out' an ordering principle for any economy operating in a world where untold human needs continue to remain unmet: at the very least, basic subsistence must take priority over luxuries. More precisely, instead of using ethical categories such as 'right' or 'wrong,' we must state that luxury needs tend to become uneconomic (that is, detrimental to the caring administration of what has been entrusted to us) when we satisfy them at the expense of meeting the basic needs of others.

Clearly, under this definition, the growth of material consumption in North America, western Europe, and Japan has been and is becoming more and more uneconomic. Our desire in the North to become more affluent directly competes with efforts to meet subsistence needs in the South. To obtain our luxuries, we extract and use up the scarce soil, non-renewable resources, and environmental capacity that the South requires to provide subsistence for its own people.

But how can this global competition ever subside? Obviously, more is involved than national economic systems: here we encounter the influence of today's international economic order, or more precisely, of today's international monetary order. For acquiring more consumption and a higher standard of living depends on access to currency that is acceptable in the international exchange.

To assess the prospect of change in the international monetary order, let us begin with the simple fact that if international trade is to continue to expand, it can do so only if the quantity of international currencies also increases. Otherwise enormous global deflation, or a dramatic drop in world prices, would occur. But how are the growth and the manner of growth of international liquidities determined? Not every currency can grow in volume in order to prop up further increases in world trade. In fact, only 'key' currencies – currencies accepted in international trade – can increase in volume: the Japanese yen, the British pound, the Swiss franc, the German mark, and, in particular, the American dollar.

If one's own monetary unit serves as an accepted means of payment in international trade, then one's own country has a relative economic advantage. This advantage, known as seignorage, consists of the difference between the actual costs of making the money and the value that the money possesses on the international exchange (just as earlier in history the value of a coin rose when a lord, a seigneur, validated it and permitted his image to be engraved on it). The United States, as holder of the most important key currency, has profited the most from seignorage. Already in the 1960s, the United States was able to invest enormous sums in Latin America and Europe, not to mention in the Vietnam War, though in doing so it also had to sustain substantial losses in gold. In 1971, however, the Nixon administration eliminated the practice of exchanging dollars for gold. The advantage of seignorage then became crystal clear. Severing the tie between dollars and gold permitted the United States to maintain and increase its already high level of consumption by means of an almost permanent deficit in its balance of payments. At the same time, countries not permitted to generate their own international liquidities, particularly those in the Third World, found it increasingly difficult to hold their heads above water.

The history of world money supply in the 1970s and 1980s graphically illustrates this converse relationship. Between 1969 and 1972, or in a period of no more than four years, the rich nations generated more international currencies than in the entire history of the world until 1969! Robert Triffin, who has described this phenomenon in his essay 'Gold and the Dollar Crisis,' notes that over 95 per cent of this expansion came from and accrued to the wealthy countries themselves.[3] Canada's prosperity has been intertwined with this phenomenon. As one might expect, the value of these currencies (that is, the price they received in the international exchange), especially that of the dollar, dropped as a result. And in 1973, reacting to the fact that they were receiving less and less valuable dollars for the oil that they exported, several oil-producing countries formed the OPEC bloc and tripled their oil prices, resulting in the first 'oil crisis.'[4]

It was the world's poorest countries – sometimes called the NOPEC because, in addition to their poverty, they lack their own energy resources – that bore the full brunt of the oil crisis, which had much greater force than all of the development aid granted to them since the Second World War. Having no opportunity to generate their own internationally acceptable currencies, they had to borrow in order to import the oil that had now become instantly more expensive. Remarkably, precisely at this time, borrowing was a genuine possibility for them, even at low interest rates. For the affluent nations and their banks possessed an oversupply of currency!

Tragically, this crossroads marks the beginning of the quantum rise in the burden of debt of the Third World during the 1970s and 1980s. For later, when interest rates rose sharply in 1979, the poor countries could not make their loan payments and therefore had to borrow again – at interest rates that averaged no less than 17 per cent (in real terms) in the 1980s. This in turn led to the reverse net transfer from South to North, which by 1991 had reached $50 billion annually.

We therefore conclude that the reverse net transfer is not an accident. Rather, it is the outcome of the highly inequitable structure of our international monetary order. That order permits wealthy debtors such as the United States (the largest debtor nation in the world) to finance ongoing increases in their standard of living with virtually no restriction. But it requires poor debtor nations constantly to 'adapt' their economies in order to meet their debt obligations. This deep inequity violates not only the rule of justice but also the rule of good economy. By means of this inequity we acquire luxuries at the expense of ensuring subsistence elsewhere.

Thus the flip side of the rising material prosperity of the North in the 1970s and 1980s is the rising indebtedness of the South. Meanwhile, the

North's increased prosperity is made possible by a built-in imbalance that grants wealthy nations untrammelled access to the world's money spiggots but refuses the same to poor nations. Acknowledging this reality may open up prospects for finding a way to limit access to the creation of international liquidities for rich nations but to increase such access for poor nations. Such a step could serve as a decisive contribution to a more equitable distribution of income and consumption around the world.

There is a final respect in which altering economic ends brushes up against the economic order or structure of today's society. In an economy of care, economic needs or ends include more than what the output of production can satisfy. They also include what human culture needs to survive: the level of care required for the environment to remain fertile; the amount of care needed to sustain communities, so that people's care for each other will acquire continuity and tradition; and adequate care for employment opportunities and the quality of work. Because these elements also rank among economic needs, satisfying rising desires for luxuries may not be allowed to run roughshod over these basic necessities.

Thus, in their structuring, industrialized societies must include certain qualitative needs, such as the sustainability of the environment and of human communities, among basic subsistence needs, and then give all basic needs priority over desire for luxuries.

Economic Means

With this redefinition of economic ends or needs, a unique problem surfaces. Realigning needs as described above means that production must serve more needs than ever. For not only must we meet the needs of the poor, but we must also satisfy the requirements of care – for the environment, employment, and quality of work. How can we meet additional needs if our means have not expanded? And does not the expansion of our means require precisely what our post-care order urges – namely, economic growth?

This question brings us to the second obstacle that society must overcome. To become a society of caring administration, we must alter our structural approach to economic means.

Let us begin by taking the most direct approach. If we add improved care for the environment, employment, and the quality of work to the list of economic needs, then the problem almost solves itself. These areas invite a sizeable amount of employment. Though directing employment to them requires separate measures, we do not have to expand means in order to meet additional needs.

This does not yet reach the heart of the means issue, however. It may seem that adopting an economy of care faces an insurmountable obstacle at the level of means. For every form of work requires remuneration or wages of some kind, and wages bring with them the desire to spend more. But is there room for this in a society of caring administration? Have we not said that the desire to spend prevents us from meeting real needs?

This issue sheds light on the more complete alteration of economic resources required. While it may sound startling, it is inescapable: if we must, as suggested above, care for economic means, including the means of production (thereby giving them the status of economic needs or necessities), then conversely society's level of material desires must now become 'means' available for meeting our newly defined economic ends. In other words, Western societies must invert their economic means and ends, so that their ends (material desires) become serviceable as means for meeting genuine need. Put in another way, contemporary society's standard of living must now become the variable in the economic model. Society may therefore no longer grant every material desire a place on its list of priorities.

Here lurks the painful heart of the 'economics of enough.' We must place priority, in the very form given to the economic order, on meeting economic needs – of the poorest, of those looking for work, of the environment and its sustainability, and of human community. But this reform comes at a price, which human material desires must pay. In an economics of enough, a society accepts that general income increases – across-the-board wage hikes – will gradually come to an end. Then, by using the monies freed up to meet basic needs, it opens the door to permitting genuine needs to enter the social scheme of priorities. Indeed, in principle, it would ensure that these needs would be met.

Our second obstacle therefore is to make present-day economic ends instruments for meeting basic needs.

Linking Economic Ends and Means

Unfortunately, altering the current approach to economic ends and means does not complete our task. Society must link its reorientation of needs and means. And this linkage forms our third and final obstacle.

In smaller working communities, the joining of needs to means is not a formidable task. A rather spontaneous link can connect the needs and resources of the community. The kibbutz in Israel has provided a good example. It is a democratic community where people live and work. Its members first jointly establish what tasks they must accomplish, which the care requirements of the community define. Only then do they decide what means remain available for satisfying individual material desires. The priority given to what is truly needed (including gathering and producing the community's provisions and ensuring that each person has work) serves as a natural limit – though not always without tension – to the amount of income and consumption possible for members.

A similar process occurs in cooperative businesses. In the Netherlands, for example, about 2,000 small businesses called MEMO companies have sprung up. MEMO companies have adopted as their first priority operating in an environmentally friendly, energy-saving, and socially responsible manner. In a MEMO, a fine attunement occurs between ends and means. Each firm's goals lie firmly planted in caring for the environment, saving energy, and producing a responsible product using the input of all of its members. The company is able to achieve this end because its members have chosen to accept a lower income than they could earn elsewhere – in some cases, even minimum wage. But MEMOs consciously cut the coat according to the size, pattern, and colour of the cloth, in clear contrast to society at large, which does so according to the requirements not of the fabric but of maximum consumption.

However they may differ, we may consider kibbutzim and MEMOs miniature economies of enough. They demonstrate on a small scale how the primacy of care can function economically in a society.

We cannot, however, expect a similar, spontaneous linkage of ends and means in society as a whole, for people do not experience mutual support and encouragement in society at large. Nor can we expect it in industries, organizations, or unions whose objective is to obtain maximum return or to win the highest possible salaries and benefits spread over the greatest number of years. In all these contexts, if we are to connect needs and means so as to permit implementation of caring administration, we must locate another manner of linkage. Here we face the issue of how to distribute and exercise economic power or control. New channels must be dug for directing at least part of the buying power provided by net disposable income to meeting the real care needs of society, wherever they may lie.

Let us first consider the micro-economic context. For people in vari-

ous industries, organizations, and unions, conscious structural realloca-
tion of buying power seems to lie within the realm of possibility. It
means that they must expand their goals to include demonstrating more
care for employment, people, and the environment, in combination with
a willingness to forego some of the income they would otherwise receive. This in turn presumes renewing the manner by which control is
exercised in such bodies, so that employees who allow portions of their
incomes to 'sit' naturally become full partners in deciding how to allo-
cate these monies. Or it presumes that the social partners set up binding
agreements which, in exchange for losses in income, settle on the
amount and type of jobs available. Recent precedents in North America
and Europe of exchanging income for both jobs and the improvement
of work quality signal a small beginning. By digging a new channel for
buying power, those involved exercise economic control in the direction
of preserving employment, not destroying it.

For society as a whole, however, the need to redirect buying power
and reorient the exercise of economic control encounters significant
barriers. For here we confront our economic order, which aims at precisely the opposite of what we have in mind! Our economic order
systematically wields power and control in such a way that they support the continual increase of the outflow of goods and services and the
incomes connected to this. As we saw above, this increase is also touted
as a solution to the critical lack of attention given to all areas requiring
care; it is partly motivated, in other words, by the post-care requirements
of today's economic order. Seeking to implement caring administration by
limiting income and consumption growth therefore includes attempting
to reverse the direction in which economic power is exercised.

We may therefore expect that every attempt to modify the economic
order towards adopting care as its primary objective will meet fierce
resistance from those who now wield power, whether we seek to impose care requirements on industries, require binding agreements on the
use of responsible technologies, or control wages and salaries through
a more guided policy. In reaction, people in power will appeal to the
perception that all Canadians, for example, want economic control
exercised in such a manner that it increases productivity, or that at least
all Canadians tacitly approve of its doing so, because they realize that
every slow-down in economic growth and technological development
will cost them dearly in terms of standard of living.

The linkage of ends and means therefore confronts us with our
most unforgiving obstacle. At least this obstacle is not technological or

organizational; rather, it has to do with our culture, with our whole manner of life and of living in society. When the chase for money and power forms the trademark of a culture, as Tawney has described in *The Acquisitive Society*, such a culture will not produce the fine attunement needed between decreasing consumption and implementing care. Rather, that culture will continue to exercise control towards what we can get, obtain, and acquire. It will argue vehemently that without this our society will die. Did not US President Dwight Eisenhower, faced with the market backwash threatening American industries, explain in crystal-clear terms: 'It is the duty of every American to consume'?

In this light, how can we link ends and means so that they encourage adoption of a pre-care economy, when the present exercise of economic power reinforces the priorities of our existing economic order?

REASONABLE DOUBT

Let us inspect this final obstacle closely, however. In reality, it is most peculiar. It suggests that, at its most fundamental level, economic power operates as it does today because all of us in the industrialized West who compulsively clutch and grab at material things authorize it to do so. Supposedly, most Canadians and others would rather raise their material standard of living than give priority to caring for the poor, the environment, the unemployed, and the people around them. But is this actually true?

The answer takes on extraordinary significance. For the degree to which such pure materialism does not accurately typify all of us – and the findings of Environics Research described in chapter 3 suggest that it does not – is the degree to which this final hurdle might reveal a flaw, an opening, a kind of crack in the wall. And where walls have cracks, they can come down. Is it conceivable that an economic order such as ours can continue to evolve towards further expansion, even after such expansion no longer conforms to people's genuine desires?

Certainly it is. At least three arguments suggest that a disjuncture may exist between what people genuinely desire and what actually takes place. They are what we call the flywheel, spoil-sport, and magnifying-glass arguments.

The Flywheel

The flywheel argument refers to the physical circumstance that when something is set in motion, it can keep spinning on its own for a long time. We have every reason to see today's economic order as something that has been set in motion. 'Capitalism,' wrote Joseph Schumpeter, 'is a form or matter of change.' Its growth did not follow a biological pattern. Rather, it sprung up as a project of expanding the wealth of nations at a time when poverty dominated Europe. Given its context, it is no wonder that capitalism became almost instantly popular. It allowed industries, in distinction from the earlier guilds, to place the lowering of costs and the expansion of sales among their primary goals, spurred on by fierce, full-fledged competition – the new element in the economic order. But if a society has organized itself thus, and if many institutions have sprung up around it, then we cannot expect immediate change when doubt surfaces, or when each round of production growth increases material prosperity. The momentum of the social order carries on, while at the same time many forms of economic power reinforce the growth orientation. In addition, today's economic order has many built-in instruments for ensuring its preservation, such as endless advertising. If we are to ensure the expansion of sales, which makes possible rising productivity, then the material desires of people must continually increase.

Therefore, like a flywheel that sets a system of gears in motion, today's societal order can continue revolving even after its initial impetus has ceased.

The Spoil-Sport

The spoil-sport argument relates to the circumstance that, even assuming that many people might want a different economic practice, we could not throw a switch that would reroute the train. Almost nothing is as disheartening as when, individually or collectively, one obeys self-imposed economic restraints for the sake of protecting the environment or fighting poverty, while others quite consciously refuse to do the same and take all the benefits. Economists call this the 'prisoners' dilemma.'[5] In the philosophical problem of the prisoners' dilemma, each of two prisoners must weigh these choices: if one confesses and implicates the other, who remains silent, the first goes free and the second gets a long prison sentence; if both confess and implicate each other, both get moderate sentences; if both remain silent, both get light sentences on another charge. It is to each prisoner's advantage to talk, but it is to their collective advantage to stay silent, and therein lies the dilemma.

Years ago Dutch economists Jan Tinbergen and Hans van den Doel used the 'prisoners' dilemma' to demonstrate that voluntary wage and salary restraints will never succeed, even if everyone is convinced that things would actually improve as a result. For there are always people and groups who, taking stock of the situation, will spot a clear opportunity to sacrifice nothing themselves but to profit from the sacrifices of others. And who among us would grant others that chance, even if it is remote? It seems then that people will voluntarily moderate next to nothing. Wage moderation will succeed only where collectively agreed on and/or where imposed from above. Without such leverage, the spoil-sport spoils the possibility of implementing a responsible economic practice, even when the majority desires such a practice.

The Magnifying Glass

The magnifying-glass argument, the most remarkable of the three, but also the most real, is connected with the fact that countless people 'represent' us as citizens at the decision-making levels of our society. The remark was once made that, when seen from government centres such as Ottawa, Washington, and London, a country's population appears to consist of at least 10 times its actual number. For all of us are 'members' of numerous public groupings – whether as citizens of a community or as members of organizations, for example – each of which lobbies government 'on our behalf.' All of us therefore find ourselves represented in many ways. However, in nine out of ten cases, it is our own material interests that arrive at decision-making bodies, while perhaps only in one out of ten cases do our concerns for the environment or the needs of the poor reach these levels, and only if we happen to belong to an organization or community for which these form a priority.

So a magnifying glass seems to enlarge the influence of our own material desires, while, conversely, a 'reducing' glass in effect shrinks the influence of the real economic needs of people or things. Not much attention therefore comes from our capitals to meet basic needs, in part because we ourselves send often entirely conflicting signals to government. As a result, in spite of our good words and intentions, the heavy machinery grinds on, merely creating more and more for ourselves.

Conclusion

The three arguments described above suggest three ways in which the momentum of our economic order may spin towards further expansion, even if the majority no longer supports that expansion. But do these arguments help? They suggest that a possible disjuncture divorces people's genuine desires from the actual operation of the economic order. And does this not imply that the direction of today's economic order lies outside our hands? Is not the situation then far more bleak than we had imagined? Taken together, these three arguments may seem strong enough to defeat any chance of transforming the economic order.

But we vigorously refute this conclusion. Consider that not one of these arguments is rooted in the intrinsic goodness or enduring value of our economic order. This suggests that, at minimum, no necessary relationship exists between what would genuinely serve human needs and what our economic order accepts as its directives.

This is already a significant insight, for it leads to two conclusions, which occupy us in the next chapter.

First, although our economic order creates an impression of enormous vitality, it may be that under the surface it is no longer responsive to the cultural demands of our time. If this is the case, then the economic order may well be internally out of date. And second, to the degree that it may be out of date, it will gradually lose its foothold in society in such a manner that it will free up ways for it to be altered at its essential points.

5

Revitalizing Our Outmoded Economic Order

In chapter 4, we observed that a change of the current economic order is at least conceivable. At the same time, any readiness to implement change in society faces several hurdles, which appear at the junctures of redefining the industrialized societies' economic ends, making the means in such societies serviceable to these ends, and linking these together and coordinating them. With the fly-wheel, spoil-sport and magnifying-glass arguments, we also noted that society may be more ready to change than we might have assumed. Today's economic order may therefore no longer be responsive to the cultural demands of our time and so may well be internally out of date. And to the extent that this is the case, it will gradually lose its hold in such a manner that it will free up ways for it to be altered at its essential points.

A SYSTEM IN TROUBLE

We do not usually hear the vibrant Western economic order described as 'internally out of date.' Yet at least three strong signals indicate that this profile is entirely appropriate – the industrial paradox, general scarcity, and the human condition.

The Industrial Paradox

First, a remarkable paradox has materialized that ties into both the care and the labour paradoxes described in the Introduction. When material prosperity increases, one would expect that industrial production would eventually reach a kind of saturation point. Beyond a certain income level, people would surely exert proportionately greater demand for non-material services and provisions than for industrial products. In practice, however, we often see the reverse: industrial goods tend to replace personal services. Service robots have begun to substitute for nurses in hospitals, computers and videos teach students as more and more teachers become unemployed, and compact discs are selling rapidly even as orchestras are forced to close their doors. Industrialization is increasing at a rapid pace, and we must understand its causes.[1]

Perhaps its most important cause is simply that industrial products tend to become less expensive than many non-material provisions and services. The law of decreasing costs applies to such goods, because the introduction of cost-saving technologies in an environment of rising production allows market prices to remain the same or drop, even when substantial wage increases occur. At the same time, as we saw with the labour paradox, increases in wages guarantee that the cost of care services in the transductive sector will rise more than proportionately, with the result that eventually these and related activities will price themselves out of the market. As a result, our economic order, whose nucleus is still market-driven production growth, has a built-in tendency to increase its industrialization, even to the point where industrial substitutes replace our experience of nature and the outdoors (as the rising popularity of massive amusement parks, for example, indicates).

The industrial paradox is a complete anomaly. Increased industrialization, which rising prosperity brings, accelerates pressure on the environment and on energy precisely as it obstructs our ability to care for people and the environment! It therefore shows us that the current economic order poses a perilous threat to sustainability. It is the first signal that today's economic order is fraught with shortcomings and is internally out of date.

General Scarcity

Closely related to this is a second phenomenon, alluded to in the Introduction. In *The Realm of Scarcity*, social philosopher Hans Achterhuis points out that in previous centuries the word 'scarcity' was never used in a general sense.[2] Of course, there were critical shortages of certain goods from time to time, but people possessed no notion of scarcity in general, as we do today. Generalized scarcity, perhaps best reflected in the enormous and increasingly permanent deficits in the West, including Canada's federal and provincial governments, is something new, and it afflicts only industrialized economies.

How on earth did general scarcity arise? How can it happen in a society of unprecedented wealth? Here we meet the scarcity paradox mentioned in the Introduction: one would expect that as prosperity increased and incomes rose, society would have met more needs, and general scarcity would have declined. This paradox shouts out at us every day from the pages of newspapers and from news reports. Even as economic growth continues and the average level of material prosperity rises, we learn that businesses, non-profit organizations, and governments have had to slash essential expenditures, events that occur much more frequently today than they did 25 years ago, when the average income was half of what it is today.

Here too the explanation is simple, but the consequences are immense. General scarcity has arisen because, despite vast expansion of our economic means, our needs have burgeoned much faster. Like the industrial paradox, this startling increase of economic need precisely at a time of unprecedented material prosperity is thoroughly baffling. As we saw in chapter 2, current thinking suggests that we must alleviate society's critical care needs by vigorously increasing production and by deploying continually better applications of scarce production factors. In order to facilitate this, contemporary economics conveniently accepts all human needs as given, as neutral. It therefore works hand in glove with our economic order, which brings together more and more means so that individuals and communities can meet these needs as well as possible. But what if, through the operation of our economic processes, the needs of people increase faster than this assembling of resources? Then honesty requires us to admit that really, from that point on, much activity has happened for no real purpose; the end result has been that our experience of scarcity has increased more than our experience of prosperity. Incessantly putting every emphasis on further expanding production is then like laying down a carpet that gets rolled up from behind more quickly than it gets installed in front. Needs in society have become floating and weightless, as if possessing no gravity. We no longer anchor them in what we truly need; instead, we allow them to be defined by an economic process that requires needs in order to continue functioning.

General scarcity is then the second strong signal that our economy is fundamentally out of date. It is no longer able to stand up to the demands of our time. It has set out on a path towards what Hegel called 'false infinity' – the limitless explosion of needs in bourgeois society.[3]

Yet an enigma remains. Why have needs increased faster than incomes? It is true that advertising is a powerful weapon. But does it alone adequately explain these soaring needs? Have deeper-lying factors also been involved? Indeed they have.

Consider the role that our experience of time plays in the escalation of need in a materially prosperous society. Goods and services require time to buy and to use. They also take time to maintain, repair, and eventually replace. Television, for example, consumes an inordinate amount of time. Things take up more and more time in a materially prosperous society, and less time remains for interaction with people. As S.B. Linder has shown, people in a materially rich culture tend to be more harried as well as more lonely or isolated.[4] Moreover, lack of time has created new markets and production streams whose sole purpose is to save us time. The main selling-point of a number of household appliances is that they save time, which is then supposed to leave us more time for other work or for raising children, for example. But does not the fact that all of our life is finite suggest that a ceiling limits what we can meaningfully possess? While we can attempt to alter this ceiling by producing and consuming more and more time-saving goods, ironically, this alteration consumes additional time. In a similar vein, a well-known computer analyst has recently argued that our interaction with computer technologies has produced a net loss of time, which he suggests largely explains the outcome of a Harvard professor's recent study showing that any discernible impact that information technologies have had on productivity has been negative, not positive.[5]

But let us go a level deeper. The French philosopher René Girard has suggested that 'desire' in Western society has peculiar traits. The peculiarity is not that one person desires things because another already has them or also wants them. Girard argues that this type of desire, which he calls 'mimetic' or 'triangular,' has been a trademark of human society since the beginning of the world. But the peculiarity of our Western society lies in the cure we have chosen for remedying the continual escalation of material desires, which intensify as people become more like each other and then imitate each other more and more. Our remedy has been continually to increase production. The reasoning goes like this: if we make more products available on a mass scale, then what one person desires and possesses another who desires can also possess. Two adherents of Girard's approach note that our society has thus clearly rooted its inner cultural stability in the quasi-certainty that economic growth will continue for ever.[6] This further suggests that as soon as economic growth stops, the whole enterprise could easily collapse, as unsatiated desire leads to social unrest, violence, and revolution.

Girard's picture is not encouraging; its colours are laid on thickly and darkly. Yet he has made it disconcertingly clear that an economic growth motivated by material desire knows no end. For if we permit material desire no other measure than that which the other possesses, then the end will never come. This too then is a signal that 'needs' are now 'floating'; we anchor them less and less in the reality of what people actually need to live or in genuine economic needs.

The Human Condition

In our judgment, Hannah Arendt offers perhaps the most profound analysis of what is happening in Western culture and its economic order. She provides the third and most critical sign that our economic order is out of touch with reality and therefore out of date. She wrote *The Human Condition* during the era of the first trips into space, voyages in which she detects something of a desire by modern humanity to escape from the earth. Modern humanity, Arendt argues, considers the earth fraught with too many limitations.

By 'the human condition,' Arendt means those conditions that are essential for people to live as real people. She identifies three such conditions. The first is social life in its plurality – we cannot be human without the other, and we are born from a community of two. The second is a relationship with the earth ('earthliness') – we are bound to nature, whether we like it or not, both in its living and dead forms. The third is a relationship with time ('life itself'). Time not only places us between generations but carries us forward from birth through childhood, adulthood, and death.

What, meanwhile, has become the trademark of Western society? We have increasingly viewed the three conditions not as that which forms the substance of life but as restrictions which interfere with our desires. Do we not consider it disgraceful to be dependent on others? And do we not find it irritating when nature begins to place limits on our desires? And do not many of us experience ageing as a curse? In this manner we transform the three conditions that make life and culture possible into obstacles and hindrances instead.

There is more, however. Western culture has learned to put faith in progress. We thus construe these 'obstacles' and 'hindrances' as barriers that we can overcome using every available technological and economic

means. The directive then becomes: let us manufacture as many consumer products as possible, so that no one needs to be dependent on
others; let us manufacture substitute raw materials if the originals
threaten to give out; and let us apply all of our medical knowledge and
resources to extending life wherever possible!

Arendt's analysis provides us with a key to understanding why the
demands for products, substitute raw materials, and health care have
burgeoned. More significant, however, it demonstrates that we must see
the explosion of means required to satisfy our escalating material
desires as a sign of a titanic battle against the human condition itself.
Indeed, what is happening with current processes of endless economic
growth is not *real* anymore. It has no roots in the human condition. It
no longer helps people to live their destiny in peace. Donning the mask
of realism, our economic order has mounted the most idealist live
performance that this world has ever seen, which casts heavy shadows
not only over the environment and the increasingly impoverished Third
World, but also over Western humanity itself. For the more affluent we
become, the more we alienate ourselves from our own created human
condition.

We may then draw yet another conclusion. Evidently our critical
dilemmas form mirror images. Just as racism seems to be a minority
problem but in reality is a problem of the majority culture, so too poverty is rooted first and foremost in our inability to deal with wealth.
Similarly, the degenerating environment mirrors the still deeper
problem that we do not wish to accept ourselves in our earthly and
creaturely condition.

Our economic order has had, and still has, many good sides – some,
such as respect for human freedom, ought to be maintained – but it sets
society out on the wrong foot. It draws people away from the human
condition and from what they genuinely need to sustain culture, and
aims instead at what is not real. It breaks apart culture and the world
into the fragments of its own ambitions. Consequently, it is thoroughly
outdated and must, with utmost urgency, be replaced.

A DOORWAY OF HOPE

We may now draw the themes of these last two chapters together. For
now we can see a widening expanse opening up onto a possibly bright-
er future.

People can hold on to illusions for a long time, they can cut loose the rudder steering their economic needs, and they can surrender to the hypnosis of always needing to accumulate more. But in the long run they do this at the expense of their own humanity. This then brings them to a fundamental choice. Arendt argues that in such choices people are also bound to their inalienable human condition. They cannot simply continue to deny that condition, for if they do they isolate themselves from their neighbours, from the earth, and from time. In other words, they do so at the expense of their humanity and of all that they treasure. We may therefore expect – indeed, we already see it happening – that public concern for the future and popular movements will arise precisely in those areas where our growth-driven society threatens the human condition itself. Popular movements often derive their greatest strength from what people are no longer willing to accept. The strength of the peace movement during the Cold War did not lie in well-formulated proposals but in the fact that so many realized deep down that the arms race could not continue. So also today: where society persistently deteriorates in a number of areas, where we ceaselessly pollute the environment, and where we 'hurry' time along, there potential areas of transformation and renewal will surface. People will make it known that things may no longer continue as they are and as they have been. They will no longer take it.

But if we believe that popular movements automatically advance the common good, then we do not know the lessons of history. It will therefore be crucial to point to certain initiatives that have prepared the way – to concrete examples that demonstrate that things can be different. Then, as a positive expression of its protest, Western society can dig channels towards an economy of care.

Let us harbour no illusions that the road to renewal will be easy. Consider again the current exercise of economic power. What does implementing caring administration mean in terms of the exercise of economic control? In line with the position taken by the ecumenical movement since its inception, we believe that it implies digging channels towards shared or 'differentiated responsibility' in society, or towards a so-called responsible society in which all sectors assume responsibility for their economic actions. In such a society, the production sector, for example, must internalize rather than externalize its effects. In other words, one can no longer assume that other sectors, such as government, will attempt to redress one's own harmful effects.

It is precisely here that we encounter perhaps our most formidable barrier. A society in which people have grown accustomed to accepting the authority of what we might call a 'double self-evidence' – the self-evidence that we must materially progress and that we have every right to transfer the environmental and social effects of this progress to other people or sectors – will not easily be transformed. We may even describe the force of this resistance in religious language. Today both Christians and non-Christians interact with the forces of scientific, technological, and economic progress in the same manner that people interact with idols. Just as ancient ideologies or religions, caught up in the pursuit of prosperity and security, summoned forth their own gods (represented by images of the forces of nature, for example), so too today, caught up in the pursuit of prosperity and security, our ideology of material prosperity has evoked its own gods (the forces of modernization – economic growth, technological development, scientific advancement, and unrestricted expansion of the market or the state). But our gods have betrayed us. They require sacrifices in exchange for providing us with material prosperity – mounting poverty, destruction of health and the environment, relentless elimination of jobs and reduction of the quality of work, and the perpetual return of the threat of war. Yet time after time we are told in tones borne up by the weight of 'self-evidence' that these sacrifices are necessary, if not 'pre-ordained.'[7]

The cultural renewal required therefore has the depth and breadth of a conversion. It means pointing our lives in the opposite direction, away from 'more and more' for ourselves, and the accompanying concentration of power, to 'enough' and the shared or 'differentiated responsibility' that supports it. We will not accomplish this simply by knocking technological progress and economic growth off their pedestals. Rather, we must make both of these serviceable to the requirements of a responsible society. They must serve the poor, the health of people and the environment, and dignity in the workplace. If we do not accept such a conversion, then the risk increases that we will replace our current gods with gods even more tyrannical. Our culture therefore faces the dilemma of choosing which god it will serve and which accompanying lifestyle it will follow – the same dilemma that confronted the people of God in the scriptures (see, for example, Deuteronomy 30, 1 Kings 18, Luke 12).

CONCRETE INITIATIVES

The approach outlined in chapter 4 may seem utopian. But in this chapter we have attempted to show that our appeal is in fact realistic.

Realism, however, implies that something is workable in practice. Is this approach realistic in this sense?

Consider two remarks. First, the comments offered above demonstrate that we do not advocate a sudden, revolutionary change of the entire economic order. Rather, we must suggest how a natural but fundamental change can occur from within. We have attempted to show that this change has already begun spontaneously in a number of areas in Western society.

We therefore advocate a 'dual' economy as an interim phase, in which the old and new coexist. During this phase, society can acquaint itself with steps towards renewal and with the possibility of implementing an alternative approach to economic ends, means, and power. An important initiative in becoming acquainted with a renewed economic order would be to invite to the decision-making table those responsible movements or bodies that bring with them considerations other than those of unrestricted economic expansion, which relate to the human condition. For example, groups active in specific fields of care, such as sustainable-agriculture and environmental organizations, anti-poverty bodies, and health organizations, ought to be involved in the making of our society's most important socioeconomic decisions, including those of wage and salary levels. In certain respects, the federal, provincial, and local roundtables on environment and economy may help to lay the groundwork for expanding the decision-making circle. This initiative could increase Canadians' readiness to move towards restricting consumption and income levels.

Second, what we appeal for here has not fallen out of the sky. Important examples already exist, both abroad and in Canada. They include instances where, whether on a small or large scale, people in various industries and trade unions have deliberately chosen to limit their own material desires and the incomes that support these in order to use them as instruments for creating employment aimed at meeting unmet needs. In Sweden, for example, 1 per cent of annual income earned by union members has been designated to improving conditions in the workplace. In the Netherlands, along with the MEMO companies, the Dutch Christian Labour Union (CNV) has recently offered to freeze demands for wage increases for a period of five years in exchange for more care being devoted to the environment and to the poor as well as a negotiated increase in the number of jobs available. The largest industrial labour union in Germany, I-G Metall, has offered to freeze real wages for five years in exchange for more jobs, especially in eastern

Germany. In Canada, residents of most provinces can invest in 'worker investment' funds. Operated under the auspices of labour federations and matched by 20 per cent tax deductions by both the federal and provincial governments, these funds are put to work in small to medium-sized companies that are relatively labour-intensive. It is generally acknowledged that Quebec's Solidarity Fund, for example, has helped to maintain employment levels in that province.

In western Kenya, under a contractual agreement with a British-based multinational sugar company, 34,000 families farm their own land, only 60 per cent of which can be used for export production; the remainder must be used for local subsistence. This arrangement has led to stoppage of Kenyan imports of sugar; to labour-intensive, low-yield farming that produces surpluses without exhausting the soil, and to local ownership of the large sugar-cane mill. Meanwhile, profits from the mill are reinvested in the community and have helped to develop an excellent school system and a network of modern health clinics. Similarly, the Basque region of Spain boasts a forty-year-old system of locally operated and owned cooperatives, a tradition that largely accounts for the region's economic, social, and environmental viability.

Moreover, in Canada and the United States, forms of sustainable agriculture and cooperative, local community economic development are springing up. In 1990, people in the small, northern Ontario town of Kapuskasing banded together and raised $15 million to rescue and purchase the local pulp and paper mill, which was the town's mainstay. Though some costs have been high, there have been many benefits: management and labour have had to set aside their mistrust, five unions had to abandon old antagonisms to become part-owners (each employee is a shareholder), the plant is being upgraded to meet environmental standards, and the mill was one of few pulp and paper mills in North America to make a profit in 1992.

In the United States, comparable local efforts are under way in both urban and rural settings. The land trust movement, in which land is purchased and held in perpetuity, especially for the purpose of creating affordable housing, has attracted considerable attention. Sustainable agricultural practices are on the increase, and applications of alternative forms of energy are becoming more and more mainstream.[8]

Similarly, in the care sector, the rapid emergence in Canada and the United States of 'wrap-around' or individualized services for children and adolescents is striking. With individualized services, youth who are severely emotionally and behaviourally challenged remain in their own home or community instead of being sent to distant residential treatment centres. To make this happen, children's service agencies break down traditional inter-agency barriers, jointly embrace the concept of 'unconditional care' (that is, they agree never to give up on the child and family and never to eject them from the service) and reallocate their own resources to create a flexible pool of dollars that can be used for whatever is required to keep the child in the community. Collaborating agencies then alter the structure of control, so that parents become full participants in all decisions made about their child (including how to use the funds), and they draw in people from the family's surroundings who know the child and family best – such as a neighbour, a relative, an older friend – and even pay them appropriately to provide essential services. Individualized services draw in the informal, transductive sector, legitimize it, and link it to the professional sector in groundbreaking ways. Significantly, though researchers express caution, comparison studies show that not only are wrap-around services generally more cost-effective than institutional, residential treatment, but the outcomes for children and youth are markedly better.[9]

In all of this, elements of a new economic order have sprung up spontaneously in the midst of the existing economy.[10]

For several years in the ecumenical community there has been talk about a 'sustainable economy,' and economists such as Herman Daly have participated.[11] But we refer also to concrete scenarios that have already been worked out. For example, in 1983 the Netherlands Scientific Council for Government Policy, a research arm of the national government, published a study entitled *A Policy-Oriented Survey of the Future*.[12] The council attempted to trace the country's future over a ten-year period, assuming adoption of each of three scenarios: further expansion of the market economy ('export-led growth'); extension of the welfare state ('consumption-oriented growth'); or implementation of the economics of enough ('stewardship,' 'a sustainable society,' 'the economics of care,' or 'the economics of voluntary austerity'). With the help of a Leontieff-type input/output model, to which, because of the requirements of the 'sustainable society' perspective, a 'quality of work' category was added, a research group of the council projected the likely outcomes of each of the three scenarios.

In its accompanying research study, *The Limits and Possibilities of the Economic System in Holland*, the research group concluded that the economics of enough would have a more favourable impact than either the market-economy or welfare-state scenarios on employment levels, quality of work, the environment, energy saving, capital transfer to the Third World, and government deficits, if the Dutch people were willing simply to maintain average income and consumption levels at their present plane (in no year was there a decrease in income and consumption of more than 3 per cent), and if they agreed to cooperate in orienting society, as a whole and in its parts, to these broader ends.[13] The latter study also explored in detail what each scenario would achieve in terms of specific policy objectives. With respect to minimizing unemployment, the researchers found that the economics of enough would decrease unemployment substantially more than either of the other two scenarios (by approximately twice as much), if the Dutch people were willing to accept, in exchange for a higher quantity and quality of work, a maximum reduction of 5 per cent in their level of consumption. The study notes that, 'thanks to the relatively painless goal restrictions, very favourable values are found for the goal variables, with exceptional optimization.'[14]

Naturally, these calculations have limitations, which both studies acknowledge. But on the basis of these and other studies, we may state definitively that the 'economics of enough' is not a phantom. Rather, it is a viable scenario. It possesses an intrinsic, internally rigorous consistency.

6

Sustainable Development

In 1987 the World Commission on Environment and Development published the report *Our Common Future*. Established by the United Nations, this commission, chaired by Norwegian Prime Minister Gro Harlem Brundtland, was broadly constituted. Its task was to define the relationship between development and the environment. The problem posed for the commission was: how can we achieve a form of economic development that provides for the needs of today's generation without endangering future generations? Thanks largely to the Brundtland Report, the environment returned to the political agenda, from which it had virtually disappeared, especially because of the actions of the US Reagan administration. This process reached a culmination at the Earth Summit (UNCED) held in Rio de Janeiro in 1992, ably chaired by Maurice Strong.

Maurice Strong, who currently serves as chairman of Ontario Hydro, was eminently suited to the daunting task of secretary-general of UNCED. A well-known Canadian entrepreneur and corporate executive (as well as Canada's representative on the Brundtland Commission), Strong has been a long-standing proponent of economic renewal. Already in 1978 he had declared: 'Our commitment to continuous growth in gross national product is built right into the economic system by which modern industrialized societies function. It is based on the assumption that more is better, that the well-being of the societies can only be assured by continuous growth in the material sense ... [But] in industrialized societies *most of the valid needs as yet unsatisfied are of a non-material nature. But industry rarely searches these out as they do not accord with traditional industrial logic.*'[1] Strong adds: 'The response of our industrial machine is to expand its markets by creating new wants and new appetites amongst the people who can afford them. We are thus caught in a paradox in which we have created an industrial system capable of meeting the basic needs of all the world's people but are in fact using it largely to foster further growth in the demand by the wealthy minority for goods and services well beyond what we need or is good for us.'[2] Finally: 'Our attitudes towards growth are at the heart of the present dilemma of industrial civilization. This is the disease which has spread through the body of modern technological societies. This 'growth disease' has within it the potential for self-destruction of our society ... The challenge we now face is nothing less than that of creating a whole new approach to the growth of our society, to the goals of growth, to the processes of growth, and to the systems of incentives and penalties which determine our patterns of growth.'[3]

As part of the debate over sustainable development, a worldwide discussion has begun about how we ought to measure economic development. Along with Al Gore, Herman Daly, Bernard Cobb, and many others, we believe that the current measure – the GNP, which is used even by the United Nations – is antiquated.[4] The GNP registers only transactions having monetary value. Sustainable development, however, requires an entirely different measure, because certain critical realities do not enter the measure of GNP, such as the fact that current production methods use up stocks of raw materials, energy, and the environment, and in many places they leave behind severe pollution, which will require future generations to lay out enormous sums. Accordingly, participants at the Earth Summit considered how to bring current production methods and consumption patterns into line with sustainability.

The issue of sustainable development is particularly poignant for the Third World. The report *The Challenge to the South*, published in 1990,[5] describes significant ecological deterioration. It observes: 'The North is responsible for the bulk of the damage to the environment because of its waste life-style.'[6] It presents its own model of development, and concludes: 'The South has no alternative but to pursue a path of rapid economic growth, and hence to industrialize; it must therefore take action to control the environmental hazards to accompany such growth.'[7]

Many Third World countries hesitate to give the environmental debate equal status with the need to alleviate poverty. They fear that the North will use environmental preservation as an argument against the industrialization of the South. (We find an encouraging breakthrough in the emergence of the Consumers Association of Penang [CAP] in Malaysia, in response to destruction of tropical virgin forests by Japanese lumber companies.)

The Brundtland Report made very clear that poverty itself puts heavy pressure on the environment. This dilemma seems to call for the formulation of an alternative, non-Western model of development. Such a model would emphasize meeting basic subsistence needs, but in reference to the categorization developed in chapter 4, it would also seek to provide items lying immediately above the absolute minimum required, such as bicycles and second sets of clothing. But production of such goods to meet the subsistence and related needs of up to one billion people would put extreme pressure on the environment, especially because of increased use of fertilizers. Thus the industrialized countries must limit their own production and consumption, to help ensure adequate levels for the South.

In 1974, the second report of the Club of Rome raised this issue. In *Mankind at the Turning Point*, authors Mesarovic and Pestel asked: 'Isn't it legitimate to ask, as representatives of the developing countries, whether there should be maximum limits on consumption ...?'[8]

The Dutch National Advisory Council for Development Cooperation formulated this need in a presentation to the European Community. Its brief stated: 'If the developing countries find themselves compelled to implement a different model of development on ecological grounds, then the need for sustainable development becomes that much more acute for countries within the European Community itself. Per capita, the industrial countries exercise much higher demand on the world's scarce and exhaustible resources than do the developing countries. We will seriously damage the credibility of the European Community's positive assessment of the Brundtland report if the Community itself is not prepared to change its own policy. We cannot expect the poor countries to strive for sustainable development if the member states of the European Community do not lead the way.'[9]

The Brundtland Report argued that we must pursue continuous economic growth in order to eliminate current economic differentials. Regrettably, it left unanswered the question of whether such growth can coincide with the slackening of pressure on the environment that is required for sustainability. But in what we consider a major advance, the UNCED conference corrected this flaw. The pressure of events helped to bring this achievement about. Specifically, as we saw in chapter 1, in spite of great efforts by many, the availability of modern technology, and a greatly expanded knowledge of organizational issues, the total number of poor people in the world has risen. Similarly, the *Human Development Report* for 1992 reports that 'between 1960 and 1989, the countries with the richest 20% of the world's population increased their share of the global Gross National Product from 70.2% to 82.7% ... while the countries with the poorest 20% of the world population saw their share fall from 2.3% to 1.4%.'[10] This situation counteracts the legitimate desire to direct world production towards meeting the needs of more than one billion poor people in Asia, Africa, and Latin America. Further, redirecting world production to this end would bring an even greater infringement on the environmental space available, as such production would also affect the environment. In this light, it is no wonder that at UNCED the representatives of the developing countries stressed heavily the environmental responsibility of the affluent nations, which are the heaviest polluters. About 75 per cent of all environmental damage is caused by the 25 per cent of the world's population living in the North. It was thus self-evident – at least to the developing countries at UNCED – that it is precisely this group that, by means of their production and consumption patterns, exhaust and deplete the carrying capacity of the environment.

In Rio, a heated exchange took place between representatives of the Third World and those of the industrialized countries. In order to gain cooperation from the former to help solve environmental problems, the latter promised to review the applied production methods and consumption patterns at home, with a view to changing them (chapter 4 of *Agenda 21*).[11] With these concrete promises, the North now stands on the threshold of sweeping change, if it can summon the readiness and political will to do so.

Meanwhile, by linking the word 'sustainable' with 'development,' the Brundtland Commission ensured that the concept of development would no longer be tied solely to events unfolding in the South. Sustainable development now has far-reaching consequences for the North. For the linking of sustainability with development implies that perhaps something has gone wrong in the development of the 'developed' countries.

As for production methods in the North, business, especially industry, now pays more attention to using raw materials and energy more scrupulously and to reusing materials. In Canada, sustainable development activities occuring within certain parts of industry, much of it under the aegis of the federal and provincial round tables, are striking. Environmental industries alone bring in $10 billion in revenue per year in Canada, are the third-largest employer in Ontario, and represent the fastest-growing sector of the economy.[12] In agriculture, such programs as the Ontario Farm Environmental Coalition's 'Our Farm Environmental Agenda' are also significant.

There has been much discussion about whether alterations in the price system can protect and preserve the environment. One proposal put forward in the European Union is for a 'carbon energy tax.' Industry officials have vigorously opposed such measures, fearing that if only member states pay this tax, then the competitive position of their industries will suffer in comparison to the United States and Japan. Environmentalists counter that it is short-sighted to wait for others to act. The Dutch environmental movement believes, as we do, that the European Union ought to raise energy prices, lower other taxes for industry, and invite the United States, Canada, and Japan to do the same. If those states reject the invitation, then the Union could reply by raising tariffs on energy-intensive products. In our view, the industrialized countries ought also to introduce a higher sales tax on materially and environmentally intensive products, and a lower sales tax on environmentally friendly and labour-intensive products (including those of repair-oriented companies).

More and more people seem prepared to alter their own consumption patterns vis-à-vis the environment. Nevertheless, because of steady increases in total available income – still the goal of virtually every government, including Canada's federal and provincial governments – less overall pressure on the environment is out of the question, while a discernible drop in the total number of poor people throughout the world is even less thinkable.

The Rio summit conference also facilitated broad consultations among non-government organizations (NGOs) active in development and the environment. These NGOs drafted a commendable Treaty on Consumption and Lifestyle, part of which we shall cite:

Overall consumption and production must be eased back to fit within the regenerative carrying capacity of the earth. Given the ecological and development crisis, this transition must be completed within a few decades in order to avoid irreversible damage to life on earth.

The use of energy, especially fossil fuels, must be reduced significantly. Renewable sources which are less environmentally damaging should be promoted.

Due to their destructive social and environmental impacts, production and use of military goods and weapons are not an acceptable part of an equitable and environmentally sustainable society.

Production and consumption of products with built-in obsolescence should be stopped; consumption of products which are transported over long distances should be reduced; and production processes which create toxic, hazardous or radioactive wastes should be halted.

Reduction in consumption should have priority over reuse or recycling of products.

Finally, we hear an echo of the themes of sustainable development established by the Brundtland Report in the worldwide conciliary process launched by the World Council of Churches at its Vancouver Assembly in 1989. The themes 'Justice, Peace and the Integrity of Creation' dovetail with the issues raised in this book. The Closing Declaration of the European Ecumenical Conference on Peace and Justice, held in Basel, Switzerland, in 1989, witnessed to the urgency of meeting primary subsistence needs as quickly as possible. It also stated that national defence can no longer offer protection and security, and it contained a convincing appeal for an international ecological order. After the Rio summit, the World Council of Churches declared: 'One important contribution that the churches can make to the UNCED process is to speak clearly to the indivisible connections between these issues, and of the impossibility of addressing them in isolation from one another ... We want to say as forcefully as we can that social justice for all people and eco-justice for all creation must go together.' Shortly thereafter, the council affirmed this statement by publishing a study document entitled *Christian Faith and the World Economy Today*.[13] Similarly, its recent authoritative report, *Accelerated Climage Change: Sign of Peril, Test of Faith*, urges the nations of the North to embrace the 'richness of sufficiency' in order to combat the problem of global warming.[14]

IMPLEMENTATION

The implementation of *Agenda 21* need not wait for the end of the century. In fact, it is in this century that the battle to banish the causes of poverty and environmental degradation has begun. The political art will be to address both issues together, rather than one at the expense of the other. The new agenda requires reconstructing society, both nationally and internationally. Sustainability and justice are at stake. It is high time that economics, both in theory and in practice, becomes attuned to the broader agenda provisionally drawn up in Rio de Janeiro.

7

'But That's Impossible!'

In this chapter we seek to answer a number of objections frequently voiced against renewing the economy.

OBJECTION 1: WHAT ABOUT 'HUMAN NATURE'?

It is self-evident that what undergirds today's economic system and economic theory is our pursuit of the 'acquisitive society.' This pursuit both drives the economy and is a result of it. The desire for more material products plays such a central role that we frequently hear it described as a basic trait of human nature. When discussing patterns of economic practice in the light of the prospects for economic renewal, we often hear: 'But that's how people are,' or 'That's human nature,' or 'People are greedy by nature.' We forget, of course, that people are also directed towards either greed or mutual responsibility.

Four arguments, based on assumed traits of human nature, are often used to defend our economic order or to reject the possibility of renewing it.

The first and perhaps most common argument, alluded to above, is that because people are greedy by nature, economic renewal is out of the question.

The second is that more possessions serve to compensate for the dwindling satisfaction of work. Economists such as Irving Fetscher have linked mounting alienation in the workplace with the drive to consume: 'Just as the body, which no longer experiences the exertion of physical work, has the compensation of sport, so too the unfulfilled soul has the compensation of luxury.' Consumption thus fills a vacuum created at work, and this then serves as a rationale for continuing current economic patterns.

A third argument is that people need to acquire enough wealth in order to safeguard themselves against potential insecurity and vulnerability. Western society has structured itself in such a way that difficult circumstances throw us back upon ourselves. If, through accident or disease, one can no longer participate in the economic process, then the government's safety net provides a minimal benefit. But that is virtually all that is available: by and large, we can no longer appeal to our neighbour and/or to the broader community. The forces of individualism have all but eliminated this possibility. Those in difficult circumstances must 'earn' whatever they require over and above that which a minimal government benefit provides, regardless of whether this goal is in the realm of possibility. Employment today thus has to supply not only what we require to meet our needs and material desires today but also a 'nest egg' as a margin against the uncertainties of the future. This too serves to encourage continuation of our pursuit of economic growth.

A fourth argument is that lopsided income distribution, together with the dissimilar consumption opportunities it brings, motivates people to intensify their involvement in the production process. This argument amounts to a social explanation for why we have increased our efforts, individually and collectively, to expand production. It replaces the 'metaphysical' explanation of poverty, which gradually fell out of favour in the nineteenth century. Society gradually transformed poverty into an economic and political problem requiring a 'solution.' However, many people also argued that poverty provided the best motivation for work. They viewed hunger, for instance, as an effective means for stimulating industriousness. The modern variation – that we must maintain 'sufficiently large' income differentials in order to keep motivation and industriousness alive – amounts to a defence for continuing and expanding the acquisitive society.

People thus appeal to at least four traits of human nature to help defend the present economic order and its priorities – greed, the need to compensate for the loss of job satisfaction, the need to build up a 'nest egg' in the face of possible future hardship, and the need to have fear of poverty motivate people to work. Ironically, a renewed economy would remove the conditions that cause several of these traits to flourish.

But what we wish to dispute here is the assumption that these types of human behaviour and reaction apply at all times and in all respects. We reject the one-sided premise that these traits are constant. Those who argue that they are constant reject in principle any appeal for change or reversal. And it is their rejection, in our view, that slows the process of economic renewal. Of course, we must have realistic expectations about change and its pace. But it is our conviction that the current lack of change is the result of neglect, not of inability. Neglect has to do with ignoring things, with refusing to see things as they are.

It strikes us, in contrast, that people behave both as genuine neighbours and as enemies. While no single societal order can cancel out or neutralize this ambivalence, every societal order orients its members in one or the other direction. No societal order is indifferent or neutral. The present social and economic order encourages people to pursue individual self-interest, at the expense of community, neighbourliness, and freedom for all. Further, both capitalism and socialism set out first to exploit the dissimilarities in people's capabilities and endowments and then to temper somewhat the excesses.

But a renewed order would seek to encourage and reward community and freedom for all. As already stated, we envision a society whose primary concern at the national and international levels is to encourage the right to sustenance of the other, both now and in the future, in which the alleviation of suffering, injustice, violence, and oppression is paramount. To help bring this about, we seek to preserve several long-standing principles and values in Western society but to alter fundamentally the means and instruments for implementing them. We further presume, given the ambivalence of human nature and other factors, that people are capable of implementing this alteration, both in principle and concretely. In short, we must seek to alter society and its economic order in such a way that they encourage all people to fulfill their callings in life. We do not propose that people, for the sake of maintaining their own standard of living, ignore or neglect the other.

None of this is to suggest that greed and self-interest do not belong to human nature. On the contrary, they are indeed enduring and obstinate. And this is precisely the point. Why must we stimulate greed and reward self-interest? Why must we make stirring appeals designed to awaken our own capacity for greed, appeals that occasionally even suggest that without more consumption our society as we know it will die? Why do we not make appeals in the reverse direction? References to greed and other sobering human traits may never legitimize our economy, for they are incapable of directing responsible economic practice. The discipline of economics has been far too comfortable with these anthropological assumptions. And we call on them far too easily as a basis for rejecting any proposal to transform our approach to economic ends and means.

OBJECTION 2: WHAT ABOUT GOVERNMENT DEFICITS?

A second objection to renewing the economy is that government finances cannot tolerate a slow-down in economic growth. Currently, massive budget deficits plague Canada's federal and provincial governments, and if the economy stagnates, so the argument goes, then inevitably governments' income will decline and their deficits will rise even further. Consequently, whether one likes it or not, Canadians have no choice but to pursue economic growth. This objection plays into a parallel argument – that the economics-of-enough scenario sketched in chapter 5 will weaken the competitive position of Canadian industry, because the costs of environmental and social care will increase.

The government-deficit objection appears plausible on the surface – until we observe that one critical issue has been omitted. Why have the governments of *affluent* nations such as Canada become racked with enormous deficits? One would expect that, surrounded by wealth, governments would have received enough money to manage their affairs well. Why then has this not occurred? And why do deficits appear to skyrocket even under governments 'committed' to deficit reduction?

There are three major reasons for the perpetual swelling of government deficits, that lie at the core of that economic malaise known as the 'crisis of the welfare state.' The first reason, briefly alluded to in chapter 2, is that government activities, such as providing police protection, administering justice, and overseeing education, health, and social welfare, belong not to the industrial but to the service sector of society. They are therefore susceptible to the patterns of the labour and industrial paradoxes. As we saw in chapter 2, in the service sector, productivity per worker rises more slowly than in the industrial sector. An educator cannot teach increasing numbers of students every year. Yet as an employer, the government must contend each year with rising wage and salary levels, dictated by productivity increases in the advanced sectors of the economy. Each year, therefore, most government services become proportionately more expensive than goods made in the directly productive sector, because the wage and salary increases cannot be recouped through higher productivity. Governments' income must therefore rise regularly at a disproportionate level if they are to avoid even higher deficits. But a society overcome by a general feeling of scarcity will hardly permit tax increases. On the contrary, most people will shun taxes and attempt to roll them back. As a result, Canada's governments increasingly find themselves running a deficit.

A related development forms a second reason for the alarmingly rapid increase of government deficits. Because the private sector orients itself to increasing productivity and saving costs, it 'rolls over' to government more and more expenditures and liabilities that it itself had borne and ought to bear. These range from cultural and environmental protection to retraining and battling unemployment. Companies freely lay people off whenever they need to save money, but, as economist John Maurice Clark observed already seventy years ago, the overall costs of these lay-offs enter society as a whole as 'social overhead costs,' as unemployment benefits fall short of sustaining the families involved.[1] Environmental costs and liabilities experience a similar roll-over. Though the tasks of preventing and fighting environmental damage belong to all producers and consumers, by and large both groups prefer to expel them from their own areas of responsibility. The government must then attempt to remediate that which is yet remediable, often at extremely high cost.

As a result, more and more costs and liabilities press themselves on government, including higher costs for medical care, driven up by modern 'prosperity diseases.' Together, social, environmental, and health care costs have helped to jack up government expenditures to heights hitherto unforeseen.

But there is a third significant reason for soaring government deficits. For most levels of government, social assistance and remediation expenditures are inextricably coupled with rising income levels in society in general. The Dutch secretary general of economic affairs, Professor Geelhoed, wrote in a 1991 New Year's article in the journal *Economic Statistical Reports* that each real-income increase of 1/2 per cent in collective labour agreements in the Netherlands brings with it extra government expenditures of three billion guilders over three years – substantially more than what the government would have received from a 1/2 per cent hike in income taxes. This general pattern largely applies across the industrialized nations. As a result, budget deficits in Canada grow with each round of income increases.

For these three simple reasons, the argument that economic growth is required in order to rehabilitate government finances – in Canada or elsewhere – is a pure fallacy and obscures the real problem. Yet it is an argument that is made gratuitously and accepted uncritically.[2] In the short term, of course, economic growth does ease the problem of government finances, because higher growth expands the tax base. But in the long term, it generates significantly higher government expenditures, especially when the general level of income in society rises to the same degree.

We must therefore turn the argument on its head. As we saw above, in the economics of enough we reorient our economic goals to create more opportunities within industry for people to devote care to others and the environment, as well as to the quality of work. We will then prevent further environmental and other damage from occurring and prevent the costs associated with them from rising. Further, this need not threaten the competitive position of industry: on the contrary, it is the present budget deficit positions of the federal and provincial governments that in principle now seriously harm the competitive position of Canadian industry. It is precisely when various differentiated sectors of society show signs of implementing pre-care, on the one hand, and of flattening out general wage and salary increases, on the other hand, that we will have opened up prospects for a lasting resolution to today's increasingly bitter debates over government deficits. No longer would the range of governments' affairs need to expand endlessly. Indeed, in areas where Canadian society relaxes its pattern of expelling social and environmental burdens onto the government and at the same time holds constant the salary component of government expenditures, there a durable foundation will have been built on which to rehabilitate and renew government finances.

OBJECTION 3: WHAT ABOUT THE ROLE OF THE FEDERAL AND PROVINCIAL GOVERNMENTS IN SHAPING SUCH A COMPLEX SOCIETY?

In discussions about alleviating injustice, poverty, and violence, the role of government quickly assumes centre stage. Many people also question whether we can really 'shape' complex societies such as Canada.

While a few believe that government must play no role in economic life, even fewer claim that the government must guide the entire economy. This discussion quickly devolves onto the degree or extent of government involvement in alleviating distress. But too often, in our view, such debate suffers from abstraction. We recommend instead assessing concrete local and global realities themselves and, from out of this assessment, determining the role or scope of government involvement. We find the debate about whether or not one can actually 'shape' industrialized societies similarly abstract and unhelpful, because modern societies carry all the hallmarks of being continually shaped. The key questions are rather: *who* shapes *what* and on behalf of *whom*?

Let us illustrate this with the issue of technology. Technology powerfully influences all of us, but especially workers in a factory. Without being able to influence technological development, factory workers confront each day the consequences of 'technological innovation' – loss of jobs and in quality of work. In this context, few consider the possibility of shaping the workplace, yet the workplace is thoroughly shaped on an ongoing basis: the employer continually shapes it in such a way that it makes more profit. For the entrepeneur, today's economic order rewards his or her own self-interest and ongoing profit. He or she therefore shapes the workplace under the contraints of an extremely narrow perspective.

If one uses the phrase 'shaping society' to mean regulating society by way of government subsidies, premiums, and taxes, then clearly the government's current ability to shape society has limits. To give another example: attempts to stimulate housing construction by way of subsidies or tax breaks often do lead to construction of new houses, but these dwellings tend to house the privileged and prominent more often than people in critical need. But one may not generalize from such flaws and omissions in government policy to assert that government regulation cannot help to shape society. Instead, the flaws must be corrected. Government remains an important body for helping to change society, but its regulations are effective only if a substantial majority of the population supports them.

Meanwhile, those who desire to set in motion the free play of social forces also seek to shape society, but not always to positive social effect. Inevitably, setting these forces in motion results in narrowing the scope of freedom. Historically, when societies have given social forces free rein, the relationship between the rich and the poor has developed in such a way that freedom for all perpetually diminishes.

Society must therefore be shaped towards an entirely different perspective. This process involves more than pleading for a general change of heart in society. It also involves the government. Though it proceeds from the belief that human beings are willing to change, people, including those holding economic power, have not always shown such a willingness. Because those who exercise economic power do not always pursue justice, one cannot avoid the use of legislation to help direct society towards responsible economic practice. Some may argue that new consolidations of power may then emerge, but this objection ought never to stand in the way of change.

Shaping society also requires more than adopting a change in life-style. In and of itself, such a shift cannot break the 'logic of capitalist expansion' described above. Adopting elements of a new lifestyle does, however, publicly express the desire to break away from existing patterns and power relationships. But if we renounce the pursuit of material prosperity without also changing current disparities in economic power, we will have little effect. Our experience teaches us that we cannot solve macro-economic problems by merely calling for changes in the micro- sphere, because such an appeal does not fully address the current wielding of economic control.

We therefore need to locate new ways of democratizing important decisions about investments and their financing. In the framework of a responsible society, at minimum this implies that those who exercise economic power must become more accountable for the decisions. The right of people to own and participate in major decisions affecting their lives deserves much broader attention in economics. We must seek mutual responsibility. And we must explore avenues for enhancing mutual responsibility, such as pursuing local, community economic development and emphasing it more in child and adult education.

Unquestionably, the abuse of economic power will continue. But we reject the thesis that it must be the final word. Instead, we advocate an economy that presents fewer opportunities to abuse power.

Does it make sense to argue for a different economic approach when such enormous power is wielded in today's economy? We acknowledge the scope of that power. Yet we believe that one can seek to alter existing power structures only after having acquired insight into how these structures work. This, of course, does not excuse any of us from concretely seeking different power relationships. But doing so becomes easier when we possess a clear perspective on an alternative. We must then think through and present recommendations for change. And we broach several such recommendations in the final chapter.

OBJECTION 4: WHAT ABOUT POPULATION GROWTH?

World population growth is discouraging for all who pursue a better situation for the victims of today's global economic system. Population increases aggravate their difficulties. The unprecedented explosion of production after 1945 has remained largely invisible, because we must divide the total production over so many more people. From the vantage point of alleviating poverty, disease, and environmental damage, the rapid rise in population, especially in the Third World, is truly disturbing.

Many people object to the possibility of regulating birth as well as death. Of course, we consider this area primarily the responsibility of parents. But private-sector institutions and governments should assist parents as much as possible. Do we in the West do everything we can to inform and educate parents? And have our churches done so?

To arrive at a balanced view of population growth, we must consider the responsibilities of the industrialized nations themselves. On average each inhabitant thereof consumes about 10 times more energy and resources than each inhabitant of the South. Seventy-five per cent of 'greenhouse gas' emissions comes from 25 per cent of the world's population, most of which lives in the North. This situation, as we see below, has accelerated population growth in the Third World.

Financial support to the United Nations Fund for Population Activities (UNFPA) ought to be bolstered by larger contributions from member states. New studies of the UNFPA show that family planning programs require more resources to continue. This is confirmed by the *Report of the Women's Congress for a Healthy Planet*, which estimates that approximately 500 million couples would participate in family planning programs if they had the resources to do so.[3]

In the meantime, however, poverty itself increasingly causes rapid population growth in the Third World. In the context of Africa, the report *Hunger 1992* states the matter precisely: 'While security in old age for both men and women wholly depends on their surviving children, most Africans will continue to want large families ... In the absence of greater access to more education and higher status for girls and women, early marriage and frequent child-bearing will continue.'[4] The primary initiative therefore must come by way of alleviating poverty, in combination with efforts to improve the position of women in the economy, in education and in society as a whole.[5]

OBJECTION 5: IS NOT ECONOMIC RENEWAL IDEALIST
AND UTOPIAN?

Opponents of the renewal of economic theory and practice repeatedly accuse those who promote it of being idealistic, if not utopian; they counter with 'realism.' But what does their realism refer to? Usually, it seems that 'realism' refers to the assumed inability of people to change as well as to the complexity of modern society. But *we* use the word to refer to 'reality,' especially the horrific reality sketched in chapter 1. We do not pretend that our proposals will simply dissolve this reality, but we do submit that their implementation will help to alleviate the suffering, injustice, and violence that that reality brings, and eventually bring it to a halt. We consider it unrealistic and even illusory to think that the economy can simply continue to develop along its current, antiquated patterns, while we remain oblivious to the consequences for people and the environment. In the words of US Vice-President Al Gore, 'It is as if the ultrarational 'economic man' of classical theory actually believes in magic.'[6]

But another factor comes into play here. We can no longer remain blind to the consequences of our economic actions, because they are recoiling upon us. Their harmful effects conflict with the nature of a just, sustainable, and participatory society. What then are people capable of in a participatory process? Is it 'realistic' to expect that they will orient themselves to others? Though they may not, they also may.

We endorse the approach 'unpacked' twenty-five years ago by Dutch scholar Feitse Boerwinkel, American thinker and civil rights activist Dr Martin Luther King, Jr, and Canadian philosopher George Grant. In a book entitled *Inclusive Thinking*, Boerwinkel argues that our dominant mode of thinking is antagonistic: 'We think in terms of "either/or": "either he goes, or I go. Either his business succeeds, or mine does." People have therefore always been inclined to group together for the purpose of opposing other groups of people.'[7] Forms of cooperation also exist in antagonistic thinking, but they are limited, and they assist one group in opposing another group.

Antagonistic or exclusivist thinking has been imparted to all of us. But if we extend and develop this mode of thinking into today's global political and economic relationships, then we raise the prospects of mutual annihilation. With exclusivist thinking, we can no longer win wars, for example; we can only engage in mutual destruction.

Boerwinkel argues that we must adopt new modes of thinking, which will lead to new action. To this end, he contrasts inclusive thinking with antagonistic. The former 'proceeds fundamentally from the point of view that my well-being cannot be gained at the expense of the other. I can have it only if at the same time I advance the well-being of the other.' He adds: 'One must not construe this statement as idealist, but as realist. Its intention is not to suggest that it is more noble or nice to advance the well-being of the other, but that it is more sensible.'

In his last book, *Where Do We Go from Here: Chaos or Community?*, Martin Luther King, Jr, eloquently develops the same point: 'From time immemorial men have lived by the principle that "self-preservation is the first law of life." But this is a false assumption. I would say that other-preservation is the first law of life. It is the first law of life precisely because we cannot preserve self without being concerned about preserving other selves. The universe is so structured that things go awry if men are not diligent in their cultivation of the other-regarding dimension. "I" cannot reach fulfillment without "thou."'[8] Significantly, he adds: 'A genuine program on the part of the wealthy nations to make prosperity a reality for the poor nations will in the final analysis enlarge the prosperity of all. One of the best proofs that reality hinges on moral foundations is the fact that when men and governments work devotedly for the good of others, they achieve their own enrichment in the process.'[9]

Inclusive thinking, which seeks to identify and serve the common good, has been strong in Canada's history. George Grant, in his well-known *Lament for a Nation*, finds that an emphasis on the common good lies at the heart of Canadian history: 'Our hope lay in the belief that on the northern half of this continent we could build a community which had a stronger sense of the common good and of public order than was possible under the individualism of the capitalist dream.'[10]

Based on such arguments, we contend that inclusive thinking both has historical roots and is in principle realistic.

OBJECTION 6: ARE NOT THE ISSUES INTERNATIONAL IN NATURE?

Another objection frequently voiced against implementing change in the economy is that today's major economic problems have become international and so less powerful nations, such as Canada, or even its provinces, cannot accomplish anything on their own. This argument, however, usually acts as a foil for refusing to consider proposals for renewal on their own merits. By simply deferring to the power of larger governments or countries, people conveniently side-step the need for self-reflection and eventual change in economic behaviour.

Of course, in many respects Canada, like the Netherlands, does find itself dependent on outside economic influences. But these are not the *sole* forces at work. Ironically, those who observe discussions under way in even more 'powerless' countries about implementing an alternative economic practice come away impressed by the wide variety of proposed activities and alternatives. It is our ardent desire that all of us, whether inhabitants of superpowers or non-superpowers, participate more fully in such activities, in order to help build up an international network of those who wish to give people and nations the opportunity to meet their genuine needs and to face the future without fear.

People must not tolerate appeals to the fact that their own country is not an island and thus cannot act alone, for such statements serve to dismiss any call to amend the political and economic order. We must also emphatically reject any assertion that because we criticize the current order, we belong by definition in the camp of those who promote the centrally planned economy. Such black-and-white labelling, which we repeatedly encounter, is short-sighted, unfruitful, and inaccurate.

Part Three
A Program for Recovery

8

A Twelve-Step Program for Economic Recovery

In this final chapter, we explore the possibilities of taking a few steps now towards a renewed Canadian economy. We shall focus especially on specific steps that Canada can take to lead the way towards an economy of care in the industrialized nations. In our view, Canada is uniquely positioned, both historically and politically, to set a powerful example. It is richly endowed with the legacy of the era of Lester B. Pearson, while internationally it has a reputation – including among the nations of the South – for adopting independent positions. Moreover, Canada is known for fulfilling its international responsibilities. It played a decisive role during the Second World War – and its soldiers liberated the Netherlands, for example. Perhaps the time has now come for Canada to take another stand, which would form the vanguard of an equally liberating economic renewal within the industrialized nations today.

New thinking about economics requires new action. Renewing industrialized economies such as Canada's requires nothing less than a conversion.[1] Conversion means making a complete reversal, or making a revolution. The word 'revolution' accurately describes the radicality and all-embracing change we believe is required. But as a description of the means of change, 'revolution' is far less suitable. For a revolution would destroy not only the prerequisites of life but also the objectives of an economy of care.

What is needed is a prophetic openness, in the sense of the biblical prophets who startle and arouse us to action, combined with infinite patience and inventiveness in stimulating change towards the common good. And we must operate out of an accurate assessment of the power that today's sociopolitical and economic order wields.

In this chapter, we offer a twelve-step program for economic recovery in Canada. In doing so, we focus not on meeting 'infinite needs' but on building human relationships that are less unjust, violent, and oppressive than they are now. The twelve steps are partly negative (that is, they outline what must be abandoned and alleviated) but largely positive.

They are also intimately related. To grasp their interrelationship, let us juxtapose for a moment images depicting two types of societies: a tunnel society and a fruit-tree society.[2]

Consider a traffic tunnel and a fruit tree. They are similar in the sense that processes flow through each of them. Each performs a function and has an objective. However, the consequences of each process are strikingly different. In a tunnel, traffic must travel through as quickly and as safely as possible and then depart out the other end; traffic must reach the light at the end of the tunnel. However, in order to achieve a maximal flow of traffic, only those vehicles suitable for tunnel traffic are welcome. Some, because of size, for example, are excluded at the entrance. Then, once having entered, the vehicle must maintain at least a minimum speed; otherwise the din and accumulation of exhaust and other pollutants become unbearable.

By contrast, the fruit tree operates under a different 'flow' principle. It uses the cooperation of every cell in order to blossom and bear fruit. But this too has consequences: it will never scale the heights of heaven. Every fruit tree displays the built-in 'wisdom' to stop growing in height at a particular moment. From that time forward, it directs its maturation efforts towards the production of fruit instead.

The juxtaposition speaks for itself. In principle, the hallmark of a tunnel society is ceaseless expansion of production and productivity, the purpose of which is to transport us to a rising standard of living, along with a substantial enough increase in prosperity to permit us to fund environmental protection, social and medical care, and development aid for poor countries. But entering and maintaining the process of the tunnel require 'sacrifices.' Because some people cannot work as efficiently as others, they are excluded from the production process. Some become unemployed; others, such as some who are physically or developmentally challenged, cannot handle the demands of the process. Likewise, maintaining the process of the tunnel requires expulsion. Because increased efficiency requires us to ignore the persistent demands of the environment and of people who have been ostracized, in a tunnel economy we find it necessary to expel environmental and social burdens onto other sectors of society, including government. We do so because we consider it imperative that the process of the tunnel continue. Finally, the process requires extraction. In a competitive climate, business finds it necessary to extract as much as possible from the services that land, labour, and capital provide. But this extraction gives rise to the need for society to remedy the distress caused by unemployment, environmental destruction, and workplace stress.

The tunnel society is therefore a post-care society. Strikingly, addressing the needs that the tunnel process itself creates – the needs of all that has been excluded, expelled, extracted – is now significantly reducing economic expansion and raising deficits in Canada and other industrialized societies. Indeed, rather than reaching the light at the end of the tunnel, we sense that we are racing faster and faster in a tunnel that is growing longer. With a kind of 'tunnel vision,' we then appeal for more production to finance more post-care expenditures. But now suddenly the possibility looms that, because society's critical needs are expanding at an unprecedented rate, and because scarcity is rapidly becoming more and more generalized, the tunnel is becoming a closed loop. Perhaps we will continue to produce and produce, but the promised prosperity will never arrive. Scarcity will appear instead.

Throughout this book, we have advocated, in contrast to the tunnel-society perspective, embracing an economic vision reminiscent of the 'wisdom' displayed by the fruit tree. A tree society is a pre-care society. After reaching its optimal height, it redirects its maturation processes towards bearing fruit for others: it seeks to provide sufficient opportunities for meaningful work, for meeting basic material needs both in Canada and around the world, for environmental sustainability for ourselves and for future generations, and for preservation of non-commercialized art and culture. A pre-care economy includes rather than excludes people; it internalizes and takes responsibility for its effects rather than expelling them to other sectors of society; and it practises restraint and replenishes rather than extracts.

But this too has consequences. To implement a pre-care economy, Canadian society must exercise the wisdom to slow down and eventually stop its endless material expansion and redirect its maturation energies towards production of fruit instead.

The twelve steps that follow are thus designed to help redirect the tunnel economy to a tree economy. They are intended to help put today's economy on track. While some of the steps build on each other, others take quite different directions towards the economic and societal conversion required.

STEP 1: RENEWING THE WORLD MONETARY SYSTEM

Injustice lies at the very heart of today's international monetary system. As we saw in chapter 4, the injustice lies especially in this fact: only the affluent nations can create liquidities, or those forms of money used in international trade and payment transfers. Their currencies serve as the generally acceptable means of payment in the international exchange, and their 'votes' tip the scales inside the International Monetary Fund (IMF). It is their 'Special Drawing Rights' (SDRs) that expand the world's money supply. The distribution of voting rights in the IMF is regulated in such a way that the countries with the highest incomes per capita and the highest exports have the largest influence in decisions. It has been said, using an entirely incorrect reference to the words of Jesus in the Gospel of Matthew, that a 'Matthew principle' operates within the IMF: to those who have, much will be given; to those who have little, even that will be taken away.

The wealthy nations have used their preferential position to vigorously promote their own interests. Without this position, the United States could never have sustained its long-standing annual balance-of-payments deficit, which year after year lies in the billions of dollars. It in effect permits itself to tread in dangerously oversized shoes at the expense of the rest of the world. But the wealthy nations have also not responsibly managed the world's money economy, because together they generated a far greater increase in the quantity of currencies than was necessary. As we noted earlier, a shocking sign of this mismanagement is the reality that the amount of international liquidities now circulating in the 'pure' financial circuit is thirty to forty times that which circulates in the so-called real circuit of money used directly in the buying and selling of goods and services. In the face of this tidal wave of money created by the wealthy nations, it is no wonder then that it is virtually impossible to protect rates of exchange from speculation. The world monetary system has gone adrift; it is at the mercy of the torrent of uncoordinated and uncontrolled capital movements around the world. Here too, in the light of this gross mismanagement, renewal is urgently required.

But it is precisely at this point that the possibility of renewal opens up, of adopting a course that helps to repair the fundamental injustices done to the poor nations. By no means is it necessary or a kind of 'natural law' that the affluent nations must hold a monopoly over the world's money supply. Already in the 1970s, several people, among them Robert Triffin, formulated far-reaching proposals designed to give the SDRs more stature in the system. Triffin and others proposed new rules for the distribution of SDRs under which poor nations would receive direct access to a reasonable amount of new international currency creation. Such rules, they argued, would accelerate the process by which the poor nations were paying off their existing debts, but it would also begin the process of allowing them to build up their own prosperity, step by step.

Proposals such as these, however, have consistently met with a loud objection. If such proposals are to succeed, then the wealthy nations must retard their own creation of key currencies. Otherwise, the increase in currency would simply cause general world inflation. And it is precisely the wealthy nations' unwillingness to relinquish some of their currency privileges that has caused them, time and time again, to reject essential reforms. For not only would they lose some of their power, but they would also retard the rise in their own material prosperity.

Yet now more than ever change is both essential and unavoidable. We may not allow the matter to rest any longer. We must cut to the quick of the deepening and endless international cycle of impoverishment and enrichment.

Therefore, our first concrete step towards economic renewal is the proposal that Canada, in a joint effort with other Western nations, such as the Netherlands and the Scandinavian countries, reduce the relative weight of its own vote and share within the IMF for the benefit of the vote and share of the bloc of the world's poorest countries.

This step would be even more effective if it were linked to a proposed special distribution round of several billion SDRs designed specifically for debt redemption by the world's poorest nations. Not only would this create a rare feeling of relief in sub-Saharan Africa, where there is now so much suffering, but it would also help to teach the affluent nations of the North to discipline their excessive discharge of money over the world year after year. It would go a long way towards a structural solution to the world's present monetary imbalance.

STEP 2: WAGE AND SALARY INCREASES

Proposals such as the one outlined above depend on more than the good will of one or more governments. Even the best political intentions can founder on a lack of willingness within society as a whole. If society itself shows no indication of redirecting its maturation energies away from sheer expansion and towards pre-care, then a government cannot move forward with a new policy. In other words, if a society does not wish to contribute to better pre-care for people, culture, and the environment – precisely by using income and consumption desires as a means to this end – then government has little room to move. This leads us to a proposal to both business and labour in Canada – that they expressly broaden their individual and collective tasks to provide pre-care for people and the environment, satisfying work, and the production of as responsible an end-product as possible, in exchange for increases in real income and profits; and that, wherever possible, they do so in mutual cooperation. Practically, this can take the form of, among other things, the establishment of directed funds, made possible by the curtailment of wages and/or profits.

The backdrop of this proposal is that general wage and salary increases make endemic all the shadowy sides of our current economic order, as we have explained. Pressure on people intensifies, because salary increases allow industry to boost its claim to their buying power; pressure on the environment escalates, because every further increase in consumption implies more use of raw materials and energy; pressure on transductive labour, which devotes care to humanity and the environment, heightens because of our increasing inability to pay for it; and, in the framework of the global economy, pressure on the poor intensifies because they have less opportunity to gain access to their land and its scarce resources. In other words, general wage and salary hikes exacerbate the three problems with which we began. They cause people to price themselves, the environment, and other human beings out of the market. Because of this, the market will become more and more turbulent.

As an alternative to the prevailing emphases of management and labour, we recommend instead broader distribution of available labour. We do not mean that certain specific groups – people who cannot meet their basic needs, including recipients of inadequate government benefits – ought not to receive wage and salary increases. But in the light of what we have seen in this book, we reject the suggestion that general, across-the-board hikes must be achieved in order to restore the Canadian economy.

Rather, together Canadians must learn to consciously 'open' the economy to the subsistence needs that now do not enter the market, needs that have care for other people and the environment at their centre. For Canadian unions, this means that they may stake claim to the full amount of surplus available in the so-called advanced sector of the economy. But they must also – in consultation with their members – be prepared to earmark this surplus not primarily to salary increases but to a number of concrete funds or objectives. Such funds would have as their purpose the creation and expansion of jobs in designated fields of care that now are either neglected or abandoned. Unions might, for example, create:

- a fund for improving the quality of work (such as unions have had in Sweden for a number of years);
- an employment fund to combat urban and rural decay;
- an employment fund to help alleviate poverty with appropriate technology;
- an employment fund for preserving the environment and saving energy;
- a conversion fund to assist in the change-over from wartime to peacetime-type production (which would thus complement the federal government's program for helping companies to make this difficult transition).

We appreciate that this proposal lays a great deal on the plate of trade unions and depends heavily on the willingness of their members. Nevertheless, it is by no means unrealistic or even outside the realm of what is currently being done. Let us consider in more detail several of the examples introduced in chapter 5. In the fall of 1992, Anton Wester-laken, president of the Dutch Christian Labour Union (CNV), the second-largest labour union in the Netherlands, proposed to freeze real wages for a minimum of five years if such a move would lead to more jobs, more care for the natural environment, and improvements in the work environment. The proposal has met with widespread support both within and outside the CNV (80 per cent of the membership has en-dorsed the proposal), and it may well open up new forms of coopera-tion between management and labour in the Netherlands. Similarly, the largest industrial labour union in western Germany, I-G Metall, has offered to freeze real wages for five years in exchange for more jobs, especially in eastern Germany.

Likewise, in Quebec a Solidarity Fund has operated under the auspic-es of the Quebec Federation of Labour since 1982. Québécois citizens can invest money in the fund, which reduces provincial tax by 20 per cent of the amount invested and federal tax by the same proportion. This money is placed in small- to medium-sized businesses that are relatively labour-intensive. Further, recognizing the debilitating effects of technological innovation on employment, the fund invests in technological development only 'selectively,' with a view towards the overall effect of the technology in question on employment. The general consensus is that the Solidarity Fund has helped to maintain employment levels in Quebec. More recently, under the auspices of the Canadian Federation of Labour, similar funds (such as the 'Working Ventures Fund' in Ontario) have been established in most provinces, with the same tax backing from both levels of government.

While none of these funds has yet specifically embraced the objectives of environmental responsibility, a socially responsible product, renewal of the decision-making structure, or 'instrumentalizing' income levels for the purposes of pre-care, they represent a significant step in the right direction. And these limitations too may ease: in an address delivered in Toronto, a Canadian representative of the United Steelworkers of America argued that: 'From our point of view, exploring new forms of corporate structure and capital investment is as much an obligation of a responsible trade union in these times as our normal bargaining and advocacy.' He suggested further: 'Rooted in their own homes and communities, worker-owners will have a greater sense of proprietorship over their enterprise, will be sensitive to environmental impacts, and to the constant need to upgrade quality and add value, and to upgrade their own skills. Workers who have a stake in their place of work will undoubtedly have a long-term perspective regarding their investment.'[3]

Such proposals may still, however, appear entirely new in many contexts. Because they ask a great deal of labour unions, and because much rides on this proposal, we add a couple of brief remarks.

First, people will relinquish general salary increases much more readily not only if they accept the reasons why but also if they have a say in what will be done with their resources. Unions ought therefore to locate these funds at a decentralized level, such as in an industrial sector, or even within a specific organization or firm. This will bring the added benefit of qualitatively strengthening union partnership from 'below.'

Second, workers can earmark funds for specific cooperative firms or organizations, such as Canadian counterparts of the Dutch MEMO companies, which are not designed primarily for profit and which, through their governing constitutions, help to democratize the decision-making structure of society.

Third, planning and conducting such experiments will help to create a new energy in Canadian society, perhaps comparable to that created when post-war Europe took up the task of rebuilding itself, despite the substantial built-in investment restrictions of the time.

STEP 3: STRUCTURING PRE-CARE

Appealing to industry to open itself up expressly to notions of responsibility broader than that of producing for the market as efficiently and as inexpensively as possible can easily be frustrated by the lack of flexibility available to industry. National and international competition is stiff and harsh, leaving little room for risky ventures, even if society wants to slacken wage and salary increases. Here again we encounter a problem of societal order or structure. Not only does society itself not promote such initiatives, but it can even ruthlessly punish them. How then can the social context behind the development of a more responsible company change from negative to positive?

George Goyder, in *The Responsible Company* and *The Just Enterprise*, has reflected on this issue.[4] It is from him that we derive our third step: in order to encourage a Canadian firm to adopt a broader range of objectives, it ought to become eligible to receive the legally sanctioned title 'Responsible Company' (or a similar label), which could assist it in acquiring a loyal and steady clientele.

Practically, this could be regulated in such a way that the joint recommendation by at least one labour union committed to broader pre-care objectives, one sustainable agriculture or environmental organization, and one consumer body would make a firm eligible. The public would expect that the nominating organizations had observed the company demonstrating exceptional pre-care for the environment, for its employees, and for the production of a socially responsible product. A regular review process and a complaint procedure would also need to be in place. Part of the appeal of this proposal is that, though designed to stimulate corporate responsibility, indirectly it would help to mobilize consumers' responsibility. It would encourage them to base buying decisions on more than price and design alone. It would also encourage the setting up of firms committed to change, which together would form the vanguard of societal renewal.

A related suggestion, while more limited in scope because it addresses only the start-up of new companies, has even deeper ramifications. In *Habits of the Heart*, Robert Bellah and colleagues argue for 'reassertion of the idea that incorporation is a concession of public authority to a private group in return for service to the public good.'[5] They link the right to establish new, larger firms to the legal form of the limited liability company, by which society at large determines whether or not certain responsibilities are inherent in the right of incorporation. They suggest that any such 'concession' to incorporation made by the public should occur only on the basis of well-formulated conditions, including effective public accountability. This would 'change what is now called the "social responsibility of the corporation" from its present status, where it is often a kind of public relations whipped cream decorating the corporate pudding, to a constitutive element in the corporation itself. This, in turn, would involve a fundamental alteration in the role and training of the manager. Management would become a profession in the older sense of the word.'[6]

We support this proposal, especially if it also applies to mergers that overstep an appropriate scale and to other forms of corporate concentration. This proposal would then focus more attention on the legal structure governing the founding of new or amalgamated companies in Canada.

STEP 4: REORIENTING THE STRUCTURE OF PRICE AND PRODUCTION

Throughout this book, we have attempted to show not only that society has reached the point where it must be renewed, but also that renewal belongs on the agenda of society as a whole. Relying simply on government measures is entirely inadequate. However, society cannot renew itself independently of government. To be successful, government policy at both the federal and provincial levels must encourage rather than discourage the reorientation of society. And steps 4 through 7 specifically address how public policy can encourage the renewal of Canadian society.

Occasionally elements within Western governments consider structuring their fiscal policies 'selectively' to enhance social and environmental sustainability. In 1992, Canada's Department of Finance, for example, produced a working paper that outlines a model of environment-economy relationships and 'provides results from simulating the effects of various tax and regulatory policies specifically designed to achieve select environmental objectives.'[7] When push comes to shove, however, in virtually every instance this form of 'selectivity' falls off of the table. When federal and provincial governments grant financial incentives or impose levies on businesses, they seldom do so with a view to care for the environment, conservation of energy, or the labour-intensiveness and quality of work; rather, they almost always do so to increase production and productivity.

Lack of responsible 'selectivity' in governments' incentive structures exacerbates our three economic impasses. When governments speak of 'innovation,' they mean almost exclusively that which is required to expand production towards full capacity, and almost never that which improves our ability to provide adequate care for people and the environment, or that which places technology in the service of pre-care, or prevention of harm or damage. 'Large-scale' remains a key phrase. Ironically, it also evokes the image of a large-scale and all-embracing government, which, seemingly of its own accord, becomes the natural but inevitable partner of large industry.

In contrast, government policy can encourage social, ecological, and energy sustainability at both local and global levels. Various governments and research bodies have provided detailed examples, with calculations showing their economic effects, of using taxes and subsidies (in particular a goods and services tax) to encourage companies to clean the environment, produce labour-intensively and conserve energy, while simultaneously slowing production of firms that do the opposite.[8] In Canada, the Winnipeg-based International Institute for Sustainable Development has produced a report, *Where to Start: An Action Plan for Protecting the Environment and Reducing Canada's Deficit*, calling for precisely such an overhaul. Similarly, in its 1992 document *Restructuring for Sustainability*, the Ontario Round Table on Environment and Economy made the same appeal, as has the Ontario Fair Tax Commission in its *Discussion Paper: Searching for Fairness*.[9] We do not view this approach as an 'unnatural' interference in the 'natural' operation of the market. On the contrary, because the market is by 'nature' oblivious to the future of the environment and to the well-being of future generations, it is the natural role of a government that seeks to do justice and serve the common good to bring the price structure in line with society's long-term responsibilities. Low fuel prices, for instance, may conform with today's market forces, but when seen from the vantage point of future generations, they encourage massive waste of a highly scarce and basic resource.

A policy of attaching 'prices' to external effects by fining those who contaminate the soil and pollute the air and water does not do the whole load of laundry, so to speak. We do not make life richer by attaching a price tag to everything. At certain key points, a maintenance economy worthy of its name will halt the operation of the money economy and encourage the informal economy. Some activities, such as improper disposal of oil, are prohibited by Canadian law. With other activities, not only must we pursue legal regulation, but government must also act before the regulation becomes official. The threat of officially closing down a company, for example, is an appropriate means of sanction when a firm steadfastly refuses to live up to its public responsibility, or to the requirements of *oikonomia*, including care for the health of people and the environment. In this respect, government policy is simply too soft-hearted and operates with far too little foresight. It must also demonstrate that preserving our forests – if we are not too late – takes priority over current and future automobile use. Price signals are appropriate here, but so are automobile traffic restrictions, such as rationing or automobile-free days, as well as stiff requirements for low emissions. For our transportation practices do not only affect us: they also affect generations yet to come. People will accept unpopular measures if they cannot deny or ignore their necessity. Emergence of organizations promoting restrictions on automobile traffic with city planners is therefore significant, as in Vancouver's Better Environmentally Sound Transportation and Auto-Free Ottawa.

We must therefore introduce into the entire range of federal and provincial economic policies, including fiscal policies, the principle of social, environmental, and energy selectivity, so that government can provide a maximum contribution to the sustainability of Canadian society as a whole.

We therefore urge managing taxation policy in such a way that it encourages the implementation of a Canadian economy of care. Specifically, we urge raising the goods and services tax (GST) on capital-intensive and environmentally damaging products; lowering the GST on environmentally friendly, labour-intensive products and activities in the service sector; and lowering it on public transit and repairs to existing products.

Such changes are not outside the realm of what is currently being considered. In its policy platform, *Creating Opportunity*, the federal government has committed itself to an initial such step with respect to the environment: 'Our first task will be to conduct a comprehensive baseline study of federal taxes, grants, and subsidies, in order to identify barriers and disincentives to sound environmental practises. We want to promote, not hinder, the research, development, and implementation of clean and energy-efficient technologies; renewable energy use; the sustainable management of renewable resources; and the protection of biological diversity.'[10]

STEP 5: FINANCING THE CANADA PENSION PLAN AND THE
UNEMPLOYMENT INSURANCE COMMISSION

As noted several times, labour in a market economy increasingly prices itself 'out of the market.' But it also becomes priced out of the market by the actions of government and employers. The methods of financing the Canada Pension Plan (CPP) and the Unemployment Insurance Commission (UIC) provide an illustration. Employers and employees pay premiums to the federal government in order to provide pension and unemployment insurance benefits for other citizens now and for themselves, perhaps, in the future. But because premiums are based on the number of employees, companies and organizations deduct and forward to the government monies only according to the volume of employees currently on payroll. It is the volume of personnel that determines a company's or organization's pension and unemployment insurance commitments. In other words, we 'tax' only the 'labour factor.'

Now that CPP and UIC costs have increasingly become a real burden for many companies, it is becoming clear that this arrangement leads to unjust consequences. Specifically, the present system rewards the strong but penalizes the weak. Consider two companies, each with 100 employees. The first company – say, an oil refinery – has an annual volume of $100 million, and it has laid off 20 employees in the past year because of increased mechanization and automation. The second firm is labour-intensive, has an annual volume of $10 million, and in the past year has maintained employment at its present level. Note that the CPP and UIC obligations of the powerful capital-intensive company (whose annual volume is ten times that of the labour-intensive firm) are only one-tenth of those of the other company. Not only that, but the capital-intensive firm reduces these obligations further by laying employees off – precisely at the time that it increases pressure on these programs. This arrangement is both economically skewed and socially unjust. We financially reward those who work capital intensively and automate; we penalize those who work labour-intensively and save jobs.

In order to maintain the main elements of society's care, and in the interests of justice and the growth of labour-intensive employment, we join with those, including Citizens for Public Justice, who argue for co-financing the social security system on the basis of capital strength, not just labour strength.[11] Levying employers' premiums based on a company's net added value provides a more solid foundation for assessing employer's obligations than does levying premiums based on the number of employees still working at a firm.

We must therefore fundamentally alter how we levy employer's contributions to the Canada Pension Plan and the Unemployment Insurance Commission by basing them not on number of employees but on the firm's net added value (that is, its volume minus the costs of raw materials and components).

This financing structure would also apply to provincially funded health care plans.

STEP 6: AN INNOVATIVE ENVIRONMENTAL POLICY

The studies of the Netherlands Scientific Council for Government Policy referred to in chapter 5 show the potential social and economic benefits of implementing the 'economics of enough.' The scenario registers better outcomes for the environment and for employment levels than do the other scenarios (export-oriented growth, or expanding the market economy, and consumption-oriented growth, or enlarging the welfare state), and it generates a balance-of-payments surplus that allows for growing commitments to the Third World. And it has the most favourable effect on today's exorbitant government deficits.

Of course, these results come at a price: relatively smaller increases in income and consumption. But in the framework of the objectives of the economics of enough, this was entirely to be expected.

The policy changes required to arrive at the economics of enough contain some elements that governments in Canada can implement in the relatively short term. Such changes would be designed to maintain or increase industriousness, but not necessarily production growth.

The following recommendations can be implemented in the relatively short term, and they are designed to encourage environmentally friendly production. If implemented, they will also bring about a substantial increase in employment.

a) Government should adopt the principle not only that the polluter must pay but also that the polluter must, where possible, prevent pollution (the 'prevention principle'). The accountability of every economic agent must form the core of a Canadian society oriented towards care.

b) Government should set minimum standards for the preservation of human health and the environment, standards that form the point of departure for establishing maximum standards for levels of pollution caused by the most damaging contaminants. Government then would use these standards to establish binding restrictions on polluters for the pollution that they cause.

c) Federal and provincial governments should alter and reverse the 'selectivity' of the present incentive structure in agriculture to encourage farm stewardship instead of maximum production, by, for example, assisting farmers in bridging the critical transition period from petrochemically based to non–petrochemically based, diversified production.[12]

d) Government should promote more intensive recycling of waste materials as well as the development of technologies that are environmentally clean and that purify waste gases and water.

e) Government should seek improvements in housing, including the capability of dwellings to enhance community and neighbourhood interaction.

f) Government should encourage expansion of the issues of environmental responsibility in the training sector, in both child and adult education.[13]

Finally, echoing sentiments expressed in a recent special issue of the *National Round Table Review*, we encourage nature-protection and environmental organizations in Canada to cooperate on specific projects.[14] As an example, at a rural environmental consultation meeting held some time ago in Holland, ten large such groups agreed jointly to invest $20 billion towards fighting acid rain. In the end such investments pay for themselves, thanks to a drop in energy costs, improvements in the market position of companies that supply the equipment needed, and prevention of additional losses of environmental values. This initiative will create 120,000 extra jobs. And the damage that acid rain causes in Holland, which is estimated at $1.5 billion annually, will decrease substantially.

STEP 7: MEASURING ECONOMIC GROWTH

Since the Second World War, it has been international practice to use the GNP as the measure of economic success. As we alluded to in chapter 6, it is also common knowledge that the GNP is an inadequate measure of economic growth, because it does not evaluate the distribution of that product among people. For example, the GNP may rise even as the real income of the lowest-income group drops substantially. A dramatic rise in the incomes of the highest-income groups will more than offset a drop in that of the lowest-income groups.

It is therefore understandable that new measures have been proposed. One is contained in the annual reports of the United Nations Development Program (UNDP). The 'UNDP Index' measures not only economic growth but also human development. It factors in several measures, such as the country's infant mortality rate, the number of children going to school, the degree of literacy among the people, the income distribution, and how land is divided. Such information reveals a great deal about the welfare of a people. The reports of the UNDP also demonstrate that such indicators offer a better means of assessing the degree of progress achieved by the development process.

Another set of measurement proposals takes its impetus from the fact that the conventional GNP does not account for the social costs of production. Nowhere, for example, does the fact that the 'use' value of the environment is rapidly diminishing enter the calculations. But a simple truth endures – namely, that when we use up our provisions, we have not become richer.

In *For the Common Good: Redirecting the Economy toward Community, the Environment, and a Sustainable Future*, American authors Herman E. Daly and John B. Cobb, Jr, present an index for measuring sustainable welfare.[15] Their proposal contains, among other elements, a measurement and valuation of environmental damage. The results show that since the beginning of the 1970s economic prosperity per capita of the US population has scarcely increased. Taking into account the reality that the actual costs of production do not express themselves in prices, the measure demonstrates that current prosperity in the United States is illusory.

Many governments in the industrialized West, including Canada's, have studied the possibility of using other measures than GNP. Statistics Canada, for example, has developed 'satellite accounts' for measuring and valuing both certain environmental values and 'household work.' Regrettably, however, these do not figure into GNP calculations, and to date efforts in exploring alternative measures have been largely piecemeal. However, certain initiatives within the business community to implement 'full-cost accounting' are noteworthy.[16]

We therefore urge Canadian organizations and political parties to take steps towards introducing new public measurements of economic growth as quickly as possible. Further, we urge the Canadian government itself to place this issue on the agendas of the North American Free Trade Agreement (NAFTA), the General Agreement on Tariffs and Trade (GATT), and the Group of Seven nations.

STEP 8: ENCOURAGING PUBLIC DEBATE ON INCOME LEVELS

Our final series of steps (nos. 8–12) seeks to address both broader and more personal issues in Canadian society at large, which relate directly to the conversion required to move from a tunnel society to a tree society, or to an economy of care.

Research has demonstrated that satisfaction about the level of one's own income depends to a high degree on income distribution as a whole. This confirms the experience and feelings of many people that the importance of their income level is relative. The same research has shown that we lose two-thirds of every income increase, because our needs level 'floats' along with our rising level of consumption.

The question then arises of what sense it makes continually to emphasize economic growth and the accompanying increases in personal income. In agreement with an argument advanced in a recent *Toronto Star* article, we thus propose as our eighth step that Canadians discuss the possibility and desirability of accepting public standards for the maximum level of earnings possible for a given job or occupation.[17] While such discussion ought naturally to take place in all of the industrialized countries of the North, it could also positively influence the debate in the South about the self-aggrandizement of the elite occurring there. Such discussion will focus broader attention on the quality of life, especially the quality of the environment, of work, and of our relationships with the poor. It will also help to deliver us from the game of endlessly introducing new products for consumption by means of securing the highest possible incomes. In many cases such incomes barely satisfy our material desires, much less the subsistence needs of others and the environment. If we introduce a public standard that sets a limit on private earnings, then we have introduced a means by which to extricate ourselves from the jaws of the 'acquisitive society.'

To this end, we must discuss and implement proposals in the direct sphere of income and income relationships. But we must also do the same in the indirect sphere of taxes and subsidies. That is, as noted above, we must manage taxation policy in such a way that it helps to remedy today's economic dilemmas. Establishing public standards for

a maximum level of income or consumption could retard the development of what Nobel Prize–winning economist Jan Tinbergen years ago
called 'non-sense' products.

STEP 9: ASSESSING 'MODERN' TECHNOLOGY

Growth mania in the West and now even in eastern Europe has reached
such a pitch that it is difficult to discuss the destructive aspects of
modern-day technological innovations. One often hears the retort: 'But
we cannot go back to the Middle Ages!'

Yet we live in a society where highly skilled labour, of the kind that
can contribute to the worker's sense of fulfilment in life, becomes more
and more redundant as 'modern' technology helps to achieve higher
productivity. This development is even labelled 'progress.' And it often
seems that employees in today's industrial society want to quit their
jobs as soon as they possibly can.

Who today is actually concerned about the person who must perform
such labour, or about the worker who is expelled from the labour force?
The science of economics has demonstrated little interest in the intrinsic
value of work. Conversely, today's economy shows little interest in
those who fall outside the labour process. Further, many economists
simply accept the ongoing development of technology as a 'given,' to
which all of us must simply adapt. Indeed, the 'self-evidence' of this
principle forms one of the hallmarks of our tunnel society, which endlessly steps up the productivity of all of its members.

The objection that arises is that perhaps we have no options available.
Because of the reigning growth mania and tunnel vision, many people
consider the argument already settled: the only choices before us are to
go forward or go backward – and who wants to return to the past? But
consider the thesis that technological development, with all its possibilities, is suited more to the image of a tree than that of a tunnel or an
infinitely extending straight line. Every technologist will agree in principle that at any given moment the technological development of a
society can follow one of several courses. He or she will further acknowledge that society does not pursue every possible technological
course, if only for the simple reason that not all such routes garner
enough financial return. In truth, technological development in the
affluent nations of the North, including Canada, has travelled along a
narrow, one-dimensional track, which represents only one of a whole
gamut of possibilities that have barely been explored.

Consequently, redirecting technology away from a tunnel society and towards a tree society – thus implementing better pre-care for people and the environment, including encouraging human creativity in the work process – becomes crucial. But this redirection can occur only after we have created the economic room for it (see step 2) and have defined the responsibility of Canadian industry more broadly than is now done (step 3).

We must also fill a theoretical vacuum. Where is the science that has assumed responsibility for developing 'technology with a human face'? This phrase was coined by E.F. Schumacher, the British/German mining expert who in 1974 published a book with the subtitle *Economics As If People Mattered.*[18] He elaborated on the approach mapped out by the World Council of Churches in 1948. The report of the council's assembly held in Amsterdam that year contains this sentence: 'Humanity is not created for production, but production for humanity.'

Schumacher urges us to locate and implement an intermediate technology. 'There is nothing in the experience of the last twenty-five years to suggest that modern technology, as we know it, can really help us to alleviate world poverty, not to mention the problem of unemployment which already reaches levels like thirty per cent in many so-called developing countries, and now threatens to become endemic also in many of the rich countries.'[19] Further, 'The development of an intermediate technology ... means a genuine forward movement into new territory, where the enormous cost and complication of production methods for the sake of labour saving and job elimination is avoided and technology is made appropriate for labour surplus societies.'[20]

With the word 'cost,' Schumacher underscores the enormous social costs of the ever-expanding deployment of modern technology in production. Modern economists virtually ignore these costs, which include pollution and depletion of topsoil and ecosystems. But they also include the increasing risks to people's health caused by the ways in which we organize work in factories and offices and distribute work overall. These costs must be calculated into production costs in the directly productive sector. If we lament the expense of workers' compensation programs, then we must also investigate why thousands of people have become physically unable to work.

In short, given the multitude of compelling reasons, we must focus considerable attention on scaling to their appropriate size the technologies and technological development that now appear to dictate society's production methods.

To this end, we urge that technological assessments be given prominence in Canadian society. But Canadians must then also muster the courage to guide technological developments to their appropriate scale. In doing so, they will ensure more labour input and thereby more human creativity and less pressure on the environment and its raw materials.

Finally, Canadians may not be satisfied simply with having the federal and provincial governments address the issues of technological assessment and guidance. This approach may even lead to mistakes, if the impetus has not come from the bottom up. We see it as critical for the assessment and guidance of technological development that firms and organizations strengthen the content and quality of the voice of labour in their endeavours. In the Netherlands, for example, trade unions have taken an initial step towards assessing and guiding technological developments – even though the emphasis still lies too heavily on scaling down only foreign technological developments. But we commend this example to all as a significant first step.

Each year governments in the West, including Canada's, contribute extensive amounts of resources to the development of new products and production methods. We urge the federal and provincial governments to use these resources to foster the development of intermediate technologies, as recommended by Schumacher. Their incentive structures should support those technological developments that reflect sensitivity to the total costs of production.

STEP 10: BUILDING A NETWORK

In the foregoing, we have submitted that today's faith in economic growth has roots in the culture itself. Our culture exhibits widespread belief that economic growth, meaning an increase in production, advances human well-being and is therefore a sign of progress. But we believe that this rather unqualified growth has not always brought increasing prosperity and that it will not always do so.

Reasonable doubt about misplaced faith in economic growth has drastic consequences for the norms and values held in society. It is our contention that humanity cannot divorce change in the economy and in economics from change in a culture's deeply held convictions and values. Economic theory and practice always reflect the intentions of a culture, and, conversely, economic theory and practice influence the culture itself.

This means that our proposals draw in many non-economic issues.

Accordingly, we seek advice on the changes envisioned and hope to involve interested persons from all walks of life. We therefore recommend the building up of a network of movements and persons who wish to embrace economic renewal. Here, in the light of our own context, we think of churches, ecclesiastical organizations, congregations and parishes, women's organizations, and academicians in many fields. Further, we must also make contacts and connections with those who envision a similar renewal but who do so from out of a different basic orientation. The search for a new humanity always points us towards each other. We speak in the hope that in the near future the peace, environment, and development organizations will strengthen their mutual interaction and networks.

An important aid for their mutual cooperation lies in the fact that all these organizations take their starting-point in what Arendt has called the threatened human condition: they seek to draw every movement away from the precipice beyond which we violate the human condition and back to the political and economic centre of our society, where decisions are made that affect our well-being and our future.

Now that we have more insight into the harshness of today's economic system, we must speak together and without fear about our own positions. Canadian and international organizations and movements devoted to care for the future of the environment and of human society should therefore consult with one another about possible directions to follow, even if that means subjecting our own patterns of life to the scrutiny of others.

STEP 11: ASSESSING INTERNATIONAL TRADE AGREEMENTS

Nations do not stand alone. Economically and politically they participate in larger blocs and interest groups. The North American Free Trade Agreement (NAFTA) and the recently finalized Uruguay Round of the General Agreement on Tariffs and Trade (GATT) represent two such blocs. Such blocs often cannot simply follow whatever path they please. Rather, they often form pure expressions of the material self-interests that they represent and of communities that remain closed to broader objectives.

A striking example of the dilemmas that emerge in these contexts arises out of the recent history of Europe. Perhaps its lessons will be instructive for North America. In 1989, we saw the boundary of stone dividing East and West Berlin fall. 1992 was selected as the year in which the European Community would collapse the economic boundaries between its member states. These events seem to have developed along identical lines and thus to have reinforced each other. But on closer examination, we detect a stark contrast. Though the fall of the Berlin Wall was a sign of the embrace of East and West, the collapse of economic boundaries, if the indications are correct, will launch a period in which the affluent western European states will seek to curtain off the East and the South.

We realize of course that others make different predictions. Likewise, the official explanations by political leaders in western Europe suggest that a renewed European Community (now European Union) will seek more cooperation with central and eastern Europe and apply itself more vigorously to environmental and Third World interests. But we question the realism of these predictions, for at least two reasons.

First, policy resolutions of this nature involve not only what people intend but also what lies in the realm of possibility. Time after time in past years the powerful lobbies of the European Community's own interest groups, whether of the farming, auto, transportation, or chemical industries, appear to have exercised much more control over de facto policy than stirring appeals voiced by the Third World, which have included urgent requests to free up imports and not to dump food surpluses from the community's agricultural production. They also have carried more weight than pleas by environmental organizations to institute a common policy on a number of pressing global ecological problems, and they have even out-muscled appeals from former East bloc countries to unite with the community. Time and time again the Ministers' Council of the community has appeared to allow national agricultural and industrial interests to prevail over any recommendation for instituting a responsible international policy. Even the most artificial tariff barriers blocking access by the poor countries have remained untouched. If this has been true in the past, then why will the future be any different?

Second, here too a structural problem plays a significant role. Since the European Economic Community (EEC) was founded by the Treaty of Rome in 1957, the formulation of the objectives laid out in the treaty has remained unaltered. The Treaty of Maastricht has merely added a few new objectives to the existing ones. Thus article 2 of the Treaty of Rome, which formulates the basis of the EEC, remains fully in force. It states: 'The Community shall have as its task ... to promote throughout the Community a harmonious development of economic activities, a continuous and balanced expansion ... and an accelerated raising of the standard of living.'[21] The goal of material economic progress still forms the heart of the European Union, while social environmental, and development policy merely 'flank' the current economic order. They possess no real corrective power.

What then must be done if the European Union is to become a just and sustainable society, instead of one that serves to enrich the affluent nations even further? At the very least, the European Union must express in clear terms its ecological and international responsibilities. These may serve not as objectives 'coordinated' with the promotion of economic growth, but as tasks that expressly limit the material economic desires of the citizens and member states. If this does not occur, then we fear that the European Commission will not have a leg to stand on when conflict arises with the Ministers' Council.

Perhaps then the European experience contains a lesson for North America. To the extent that NAFTA does not possess clear, minimum social and environmental provisions – expressly limiting the material economic desires of North Americans – the economic processes stimulated by NAFTA will run roughshod over sound environmental and social policies. The reason is that the countries with the lowest environmental and social standards will hold the competitive advantage! This phenomenon is known as ecological and social 'dumping.' The competitive advantage will then exert downward pressure on the social and environmental standards that already exist in member states. These dynamics show that the formation of international trading blocs built for the primary purpose of material advancement is irresponsible in our time.

We therefore fully endorse Al Gore's proposal that 'governments should require the incorporation of standards to protect the environment in treaties and international agreements,' with the proviso that social standards be included.[22]

In general, at the outset, Canadians ought to test every new form of political and economic cooperation with the criteria of social and environmental sustainability and of a genuine openness to participation by 'weaker' states. If they do not do so, then any new forms of international economic cooperation will inevitably assist only in closing the loop of the tunnel society.

STEP 12: LIFESTYLE

If a single theme has characterized this book, it is that if we are to resolve today's pressing local and global economic impasses, then our actions and ways of life must change. Thus it is no accident that we conclude our series of steps with an appeal to alter lifestyle. This appeal is not the same as simply taking on certain social obligations on behalf of others and our immediate environment. Rather, it entails developing a way of life that is content with 'enough' and that demonstrates this contentment by conscious acceptance of a level of income and consumption that does not escalate.

Let us therefore state most emphatically that the appeal to alter our lifestyle does not consist of urging us to make painful 'sacrifices' for the sake of others. On the contrary, our appeal is fundamentally different in principle. It involves the realization that, owing to our collective drive for 'more and more,' we directly damage our own well-being. In this context, it is illuminating to note that our word 'luxury' is derived from the Latin word *luxatio*, which means 'dislocation,' as in the dislocation of an arm or a joint. Indeed, we require another vision of life, in which the word 'enough' plays a positive role. Implementation of such a vision will create new possibilities for neighbourliness, for demonstrating care for our surroundings, and for having more time available in our harried lives. Such a vision will help to liberate not only the poor, but also the rich.

In this respect, the consumption patterns of many people in Canada and the West deserve more attention. The need for responsible consumption remains. Of course, lifestyle issues contain a personal element. But they also speak to the responsibility we hold in common for the consumption patterns of our culture. Fashion, for example, exercises considerable influence in many areas today, not just clothing. Resisting certain fashion tendencies is a matter not just of personal consumption but also of group and societal consumption. We must develop fashion practices other than those forced on us by advertising and commerce.

Similarly, the peculiar passion by which many of us undermine our own health by using tobacco or alcohol (a passion often rooted in societal problems) carries over into our eating habits. Eating disorders, such as bulimia and anorexia, plague only affluent societies, and they have mushroomed in our time. Binswanger and his Swiss colleagues have shown that eating practices today are a form of premature depletion of our bodies. According to estimates, Germany pays 3 billion marks each year in social assistance for diseases that relate in some way to unhealthy nourishment. The problem in Canada and the West is over-eating.

We also need to address the increasing lack of time in our busy lives.

Many people seem to have lost the realization that continually expanding levels of consumption put greater pressure on the time available to us, because more consumption means that more of our time is tied up with products and goods. But if we wish to live in a culture in which human contact has a central place (indeed, this is a singular condition for the preservation of any culture), then we must free up some of the time that we now increasingly use with products and goods. The well-being of people therefore is not strictly linked with expanding our possessions, and when an industrialized culture such as Canada's continually opts to elevate its material prosperity, it does so at the expense of the increasing loneliness and isolation of its members. People simply have less time for each other.

Therefore, in all areas, including education, we urge Canadians to promote the notion that human well-being, both of oneself and others, requires first and foremost a lifestyle of restraint, not luxury. And to achieve a sustainable economy, we, as consumers, must fight the 'throw-away' mentality and put value on second-hand goods.

CONCLUSION

A sense of abundance can arise only if we have a sense of enough, for abundance is the awareness of having more than enough. Yet in the realm of scarcity in which we live, it is precisely this awareness of abundance that is steadily eroding. Perhaps taking steps in the direction of an economy of care, or an economy of enough, will help us to regain this diminishing sense of abundance.

Together, these twelve steps outline a way or path to follow. They need not be taken in the precise order described here, and they leave room for all sorts of variations. But considered as a whole, they help to define a movement that draws us away from the dark abyss that society is now perilously approaching. The path outlined here – together with whatever amendments and changes are appropriate – therefore cannot be lightly dismissed. For it implies a choice, a choice moving in a line that stands in explicit contrast to the ongoing, deadly cycle of self-enrichment and self-destruction. At its most basic level, it contains a choice for life itself, and for the One who has given all of us life.

Notes

1 Roche outlined these proposals in *A Bargain for Humanity: Global Security by 2000* (Edmonton: University of Alberta Press 1993).

INTRODUCTION

1 Laidlaw Foundation, 'Canada and Its Children,' *Children and Their Prospects* 1 (fall 1993), 11.
2 Citizens for Public Justice, 'Getting Our House in Order' (Toronto 1993), 5.
3 Laidlaw Foundation, 'Canada and Its Children,' 1.
4 Bread for the World Institute on Hunger and Development, *Hunger 1993: Uprooted People* (Washington, DC, 1992), 107.
5 Ibid, 107.
6 Ibid, 154. These figures come from the US Department of Commerce.
7 As reported in *Alternatives: Perspectives on Society and Development* 20 no. 1 (Nov./Dec. 1993), 3.
8 Juliet Schor, *The Overworked American: The Unexpected Decline of Leisure* (New York: Basic Books 1991).
9 Armine Yalnizyan, 'Defining Social Security, Defining Ourselves: Why We Need to Change Our Thinking before It's Too Late,' The Canadian Centre for Policy Alternatives, May 1993, 6–8.

CHAPTER 1: Poverty, Environmental Degradation, and Unemployment

1 The title of a 1955 address by Queen Juliana of the Netherlands.

2 World Bank, *World Development Report 1992: Development and the Environ-ment* (Oxford: Oxford University Press 1991), 32.

3 Ibid, 30.

4 Bread for the World, *Hunger 1992* (Washington, DC, 1991), 7.

5 Jan H. Boer, ed, *The Church and External Debt* (Jos, Nigeria: Institute of Church and Society 1992), 93.

6 Ibid, 93.

7 United Nations Development Program (UNDP), *Human Development Report 1992* (Oxford: Oxford University Press 1992), 3.

8 Ibid, 3.

9 Duncan Cameron, 'Reforming Liberals: It's the Economy, Not Social Policy, That Needs to Be Reformed,' *Canadian Forum* (April 1994), 10.

10 Quoted in Bread for the World, *Hunger 1992: Second Annual Report on the State of World Hunger* (Washington, DC, 1991), 162.

11 John R. Evans, 'Our Consumption Is a World Problem,' *Toronto Star*, 13 Dec. 1993, A17.

12 The Bread for the World Institute considered the issue of uprooted people so critical that it devoted its entire *Hunger 1993* report to it.

13 UNDP, *Human Development Report 1992*, 11.

14 This calculation is based on the real interest rate effectively paid during the 1980s, namely 17 per cent.

15 See Michael Moffit, *The World's Money: International Banking from Bretton Woods to the Brink of Insolvency* (New York: Simon and Schuster 1983).

16 UNDP, *Human Development Report 1992*, 6–7.

17 See Clyde Sanger and Ann Weston, 'Canada and North-South Issues' (Ottawa: North-South Institute), 42.

18 For further details, see Percy Mistry, *African Debt Revisited: Procrastination or Progress? Forum on Debt and Development* (The Hague 1991).

19 UNDP, *Human Development Report 1992*, 4.

20 Ibid, 52.

21 See Susan George, *A Fate Worse Than Debt* (New York: Penguin Books 1988), part II.

22 In the same vein, Brazil and Mexico have had to cut health budgets to 25 per cent of their 1972 levels; Boer, ed, *The Church and External Debt*, 95.

23 Jodi Jacobson estimates the total number of environmental refugees in the world today to be more than 10 million (in her contribution to Bread for the World, *Hunger 1993*, 66).

24 In the case of the Philippines, this of course does not tell the whole story. The average life expectancy there has increased by ten years dur-ing the last three decades, and the adult literacy rate grew to 92 per cent

of the population. However, these averages may never be used to justify the misery and poverty that virtually destroy the poorest segments of the population and which, to a large degree, are the direct consequence of the extremely high debt owed to foreign creditors.

25 *Maseru Declaration on the Debt Crisis As It Affects Human Rights*, reprinted in Boer, ed, *The Church and External Debt*, 207.

26 Consider, for example, Willy Brandt's reports *North-South: A Programme for Survival* (Cambridge, Mass.: MIT Press 1980) and *Common Crisis North-South: Cooperation for World Recovery* (Cambridge, Mass.: MIT Press 1983).

27 Maurice F. Strong, 'Beyond Rio: A New Role For Canada,' O.D. Skelton Memorial Lecture (Ottawa: External Affairs and International Trade Canada), 11–12. The address was delivered in Vancouver on 10 November 1992.

28 UNDP, *Human Development Report 1992*, 51.

29 Ibid, 51.

30 Dennis Meadows et al., *The Limits to Growth* (New York: New American Library 1972).

31 Nicholas A. Robinson, ed, *Agenda 21 and the UNCED Proceedings* (New York: Oceana Publications, 1992).

32 World Resources Institute, *The 1993 Information Please Environmental Almanac* (New York: Houghton Mifflin 1993), 303.

33 Ibid, 303. Scientists have been aided in these investigations by data collected at the World Ozone Data Centre, operated by Canada since 1960.

34 Environment Canada, *The State of Canada's Environment* (Ottawa: Ministry of Supply and Services Canada 1991), 23-18, Box 23.2.

35 Taken from Marc Lappé, *Chemical Deception: The Toxic Threat to Health and the Environment* (San Francisco: Sierra Club Books 1991), 51.

36 Ibid, 308.

37 The citation is from *Earthkeeper: Canada's Environmental Magazine*, 4 no. 3 (Feb./March 1994), 8. According to a report recently released by the Canadian Global Change Program of the Royal Society of Canada (the COGGER Report), the barriers to meeting these commitments 'are not economic but political' (ibid, 8).

38 World Resources Institute, *1993 Information*, 313.

39 Ibid, 313.

40 Ontario Round Table on Environment and Economy, *Restructuring for Sustainability* (Toronto: September 1992), xiv.

41 All these statistics come from Environment Canada, *The State of Canada's Environment*, 22-8, Table 22.1.

42 Ibid, 22-9, Figure 22.3.

43 *Earthkeeper* 4 no. 4 (April/May, 1994), 25.

44 Cited in Doug MacDonald, *The Politics of Pollution: Why Canadians Are Failing Their Environment* (Toronto: McClelland & Stewart 1991), 296.

45 *Earthkeeper* 4 no. 4 (April/May, 1994), 25.

46 Environment Canada, 'State of the Environment Reporting' no. 10 (July 1993), 3.

47 World Resources Institute, *1993 Information*, 79–80. The US Department of Transportation estimates that in 1989 'congestion on interstate highways caused 8 billion hours in delay and tens of billions of dollars in wasted fuel and productivity. By the end of the year 2000 ... these delays on the nation's highways could increase fourfold.'

48 Worldwatch Institute, *State of the World 1991* (New York: W.W. Norton 1991), 58.

49 Environment Canada, *The State of Canada's Environment*, 24-1 and 12-16.

50 MacDonald, *The Politics of Pollution*, 260.

51 Canadian automobiles alone emit 392,077 tonnes of nitrogen oxide into the air each year (ibid, 296); the Quebec figure comes from Environment Canada, 'State of the Environment Reporting' no. 10 (July 1993), 3.

52 Environment Canada, *The State of Canada's Environment*, 12-16.

53 As reported in Warner Troyer, *Preserving Our World: A Consumer's Guide to the Brundtland Report*, Foreword by Gro Brundtland (Toronto: Warglen International Communications 1990), 74.

54 World Resources Institute, *1993 Information*, 96.

55 Ibid.

56 Worldwatch Institute, *State of the World 1993* (New York: W.W. Norton 1991), 6.

57 This is derived from a World Wildlife Fund estimate, as reported in Julie Aboucher, 'Canada and the Biodiversity Convention,' *Alternatives* 20 no. 1, 20.

58 See Environment Canada, *The State of Canada's Environment*, chaps. 6 and 26.

59 Ibid, 21-7.

60 MacDonald, *The Politics of Pollution*, 260.

61 As noted in ibid, 296.

62 The quotation is from ibid, 149. See also Environment Canada, *The State of Canada's Environment*, 21-22.

63 Ibid, 21-13.

64 The estimate is found in MacDonald, *The Politics of Pollution*, 27. Even with more stringent regulatory requirements in the United States, indus-

tries there release 9 million tonnes of toxic chemicals annually; cited in Barry Commoner, *Making Peace with the Planet* (New York: Pantheon Books 1990), 31.

65 Ibid.

66 International Institute for Sustainable Development (IISD), *Where to Start: An Action Plan for Protecting the Environment and Reducing Canada's Deficit* (Winnipeg: IISD 1994), 13–14.

67 Ibid, 14.

68 The first figure comes from Garry Lawrence Fairbairn, *Will the Bounty End?: The Uncertain Future of Canada's Food Supply* (Saskatoon: Western Producer Prairie Books 1984), 18; the second, from IISD, *Where to Start*, 14.

69 The estimate comes from the Senate Standing Committee on Agriculture, Forestry and Fisheries Report *Soils at Risk* (Ottawa, 1984).

70 Canada's soil erosion rates are not as dramatic as those of the United States, where erosion is now higher than at the time of the Dustbowl. In Iowa, the weight of topsoil losses is five times greater than the weight of grain harvested, and in the state of Washington, it is twenty times greater; Wendell Berry, *What Are People For?* (San Francisco: North Point Press 1990), 124. Yet the problem is no less severe in Canada, because soil levels are considerably thinner and much more land space is unsuitable for farming.

71 Environment Canada, *The State of Canada's Environment*, 9-1.

72 Ibid, 9-14.

73 Commoner, *Making Peace*, 51

74 See 'Breast Cancer: The Missing Link,' *Harrowsmith* no. 114 (March 1994), 31-2.

75 Terry Pugh, 'Index on Farming,' *Canadian Forum* 70 no. 805 (Dec. 1991), 32.

76 In *Making Peace*, Commoner calculates that between 1950 and 1987 the productivity of agricultural chemicals decreased by 69 per cent (p. 86).

77 As noted in Terry Pugh, ed, *Fighting the Farm Crisis* (Saskatoon: Fifth House 1987), 14.

78 Wendell Berry, *Home Economics* (San Francisco: North Point Press 1987), 129.

79 Wendell Berry has said about a specific context, 'The introduction of industrial technology ... involves a gross simplification of the agriculture itself as well as a drastic complication of the economy. It requires a cash economy and credit [and favours] the larger producer.' *The Unsettling of America: Culture and Agriculture* (New York: Avon Books 1977), 178.

80 See Berry, *Unsettling*, 194, and Commoner, *Making Peace*, 97.

81 *Alternatives* 18 no. 3 (Jan./Feb. 1992), 3.
82 UNDP, *Urban Air Pollution* (New York: United Nations 1991), Foreword.
83 World Bank, *World Development Report 1992*, 16.
84 Ibid, 171.
85 World Commission on Environment and Development, *Our Common Future* (Oxford: Oxford University Press 1987).
86 IISD, *Where to Start*, 13.
87 Bread for the World, *Hunger 1993*, 65.
88 World Resources Institute, *1993 Information*, 328–9.
89 See, for example, Fergus Watt, 'Ratifying the Law of the Sea: No More Excuses,' *Globe and Mail*, 1 March 1994, A19; Clyde Sawyer, 'Law of the Sea: A Canadian Opportunity,' *International Perspectives* 16 no. 1 (Jan./Feb. 1988), 8–10; Donald McRae and Gordon Munro, eds, *Canadian Oceans Policy: National Strategies and the New Law of the Sea* (Vancouver: University of British Columbia Press 1989); and Elizabeth Riddell-Dixon, *Canada and the International Seabed: Domestic Determinants and External Constraints* (Montreal: McGill-Queen's University Press 1989).
90 *Creating Opportunity: The Liberal Plan for Canada* (Ottawa: Liberal Party of Canada 1993), 70.
91 The first statistic is from Environment Canada, *The State of Canada's Environment*, 12-30 (with figures from the OECD), the second is from Environment Canada, 'State of the Environment Reporting' no. 10 (July 1993), 1, as noted in British Columbia's *State of the Environment Report*.
92 World Resources Institute, *1993 Information*, 70.
93 Environment Canada, *The State of Canada's Environment*, 12-1.
94 Boyce Richardson, *Time to Change* (Ottawa: Canadian Institute for International Peace and Security 1990), 14–15.
95 Gore, *Earth in the Balance* (New York: Houghton Mifflin 1992), 245.
96 MacDonald, *The Politics of Pollution*, 18.
97 Economic Council of Canada, *Good Jobs, Bad Jobs* (Ottawa: Canadian Government Publishing Centre 1990), 11.
98 Judith Maxwell, 'Globalization and Family Security,' *Family Security in Insecure Times* (Ottawa: National Forum on Family Security 1993), 29
99 Hannah Arendt, *The Human Condition* (Chicago: University of Chicago Press 1958), 5.
100 Armine Yalnizyan, 'Defining Social Security, Defining Ourselves,' Canadian Centre for Policy Alternatives, May 1993, 7.
101 L.U. de Sitter, *Op Weg Naar Nieuwe Fabrieken en Kantoren* (Towards New Factories and Offices) (Deventer: Kluwer 1981).
102 Ibid.

103 Economic Council, *Good Jobs, Bad Jobs*, 18.

104 E.F. Schumacher, *Small Is Beautiful* (London: Abacus 1974), 126.

105 Arendt, *The Human Condition*, 4.

106 Ibid, 5.

107 World Resources Institute, *1993 Information*, 79.

108 Bread for the World, *Hunger 1992*, 116, 119.

109 United Nations, Report of the Secretary-General, *The Relationship between Disarmament and Development*, Study Series 5, 1982.

110 Jan Tinbergen and Dietrich Fischer, *Warfare and Welfare: Integrating Security Policy into Socio-Economic Policy* (New York: St Martin's Press 1987).

111 World Commission on Environment and Development, *Our Common Future*, 4.

CHAPTER 2: Risky Calculations

1 Quoted by Andrew Skinner in his Introduction to Adam Smith, *The Wealth of Nations* (Harmondsworth: Penguin Books 1970), 27.

2 For more detailed discussion of the issues raised in this section, see Bob Goudzwaard, *Capitalism and Progress: A Diagnosis of Western Society*, trans and ed Josina van Nuis Zylstra (Toronto: Wedge Publishing Foundation; Grand Rapids, Mich.: William B. Eerdmans Publishing 1979).

3 R. Strigl, *Die Ökonomische Kategorieën und die Organisation der Wirtschaft* (Jena: Gustav Fischer 1923).

4 See Richard H. Tawney, *The Acquisitive Society* (Brighton: Wheatsheaf 1982).

5 John Hicks, *Causality in Economics* (Oxford: Blackwell 1979), 7.

6 See Fred Hirsch, *Dilemmas of Liberal Democracies: Studies in Fred Hirsch's Social Limits to Growth*, ed Adrian Ellis and Krishan Kumar (London: Tavistock Publications 1983); Herman E. Daly, *Steady State Economics* (Washington, DC: Island Press 1991); and Herman E. Daly and John B. Cobb, *For the Common Good: Redirecting the Economy toward Community, the Environment, and a Sustainable Future* (Boston, Mass.: Beacon Press 1989).

CHAPTER 3: Reclaiming People and Their Needs

1 These discussions, together with commentary, were published in *Over de grenzen: de maatschappelijke verantwoordelijkheid van transnationale ondernemingen* (Over the Limits: The Social Responsibility of Transnational Corporations) (Voorburg 1984).

2 Doug Miller, 'Canadians Ahead Again,' *Jobs and the Environment: National Round Table Review* (fall 1993), 35.

3 Ibid, 35 (emphasis ours).

4 Ibid, 35.

5 Jürgen Moltmann, *The Church in the Power of the Spirit* (New York: Harper & Row 1980), 79.

6 Allan Boesak, 'God van de armen' (God of the Poor), in *Met de Moed der Hoop, Opstellen Aangeboden aan dr. C.F. Beyers Naudé* (Encouraged by Hope: Essays Dedicated to Dr C.F. Beyers Naudé) (Baarn: Bosch, Baarn en Keuning 1985), 73.

7 Wendell Berry, *What Are People For?* (San Francisco: North Point Press 1990), 124.

8 As reported in *SOL: The Voice of Renewable Energy in Canada* no. 90 (Sept./Oct. 1992), 2. The project is a joint effort on the part of Ontario Hydro, the Ontario Ministry of Energy, and the federal Ministry of Energy, Mines and Resources.

9 As reported in Joel Davidson, *The New Solar Electric Home: The How-to Photovoltaic Handbook* (Ann Arbor, Mich.: AATEC Publications 1990), 13. The author calls for a ten-year national effort towards research and application of photovoltaics, similar to the effort to land astronauts on the moon.

10 Michael Grätzel, 'Low Cost Solar Cells,' in *The World and I* 8 no. 2 (Feb. 1993), 228–35.

11 Al Gore, *Earth in the Balance* (New York: Houghton Mifflin 1992), 330.

12 *Canadian Geographic* 114 no. 2 (March/April 1994), 12.

13 Armine Yalnizyan, 'Defining Social Security, Defining Ourselves: Why We Need to Change Our Thinking Before It's Too Late,' 2.

14 Bread for the World Institute On Hunger and Development, *Hunger 1993: Uprooted People*, 1992, 11.

15 Environment Canada, *The State of Canada's Environment*, 12–32 (emphasis ours). The report also notes: 'The influence of fossil fuels is so pervasive that it makes it difficult even to conceive what a post–fossil fuel future would look like' (12–32).

16 Herman Daly, 'The Ecological and Moral Necessity for Limiting Economic Growth,' in Roger S. Shinn, ed, *Faith and Science in an Unjust World* (Geneva: WCC Publications 1980), 217.

CHAPTER 4: Renewing the Economic Order

1 As reported in the *Toronto Star* 21 August 1992, 23.

2 Herman E. Daly and John B. Cobb, *For the Common Good* (Boston: Beacon Press 1989), 44.

3 Robert Triffin, 'Gold and the Dollar Crisis: Yesterday and Tomorrow,' *Essays in International Finance* 132 (Dec. 1978).

4 As described in *Idols of Our Time*, the Western nations reacted in three ways to the oil crisis. First, they made new money! In the next three years, from 1972 to 1975, world money reserves doubled (Triffin, 'Gold and the Dollar Crisis,' 4). Second, they borrowed enormous sums from the oil countries, which had become instantly rich. And third, they increased exports, largely from the most technologically advanced sector of the economy: weapons production. In one year, 1973–4, US weapons exports doubled from $4 billion to $8 billion, thereby raising the weapons ceiling in the world as a whole. The combined effect of these reactions led to the second energy crisis of 1978, which skewed the Western balance of payments even more seriously than the first. From 1978 on, the repeated shock therapy essentially decelerated Western economic growth, as the burden of debt and government deficits reached hitherto unknown heights. Bob Goudzwaard, *Idols of Our Time*, trans Mark Vander Vennen (Downer's Grove, Ill.: Inter-Varsity Press 1984), 88–91.

5 See Mancur Olson, *The Logic of Collective Action: Public Goods and the Theory of Groups* (Cambridge, Mass.: Harvard University Press 1965).

CHAPTER 5: Revitalizing Our Outmoded Economic Order

1 Dutch economist S.D. Eikelboom named this paradox in a dissertation at Erasmus University entitled 'De Industriële Paradox' (1987).

2 Hans Achterhuis, *Het Rijk van de Schaarste: van Thomas Hobbes tot Michel Foucault* (The Realm of Scarcity: From Thomas Hobbes to Michel Foucault) (Baarn: Ambo 1988).

3 Georg Wilhelm Friederich Hegel, *The Philosophy of Right*, trans with notes by T.M. Knox (Chicago: Encyclopedia Britannica 1955).

4 S.B. Linder, *The Harried Leisure Class* (New York: Columbia University Press 1970).

5 Stephen Levy, 'The Case of Purloined Productivity,' *MacWorld* 10 no. 3 (March 1993) 57–60. The irony is not lost on the author that industry introduced information technologies largely to save time and increase productivity.

6 Paul Dumouchel and Jean Pierre Dupey, *L'enfer des Choses: René Girard et la logique de l'économie* (Paris: Seuil 1979).

7 For more extensive discussion of this theme, see Goudzwaard, *Idols of Our Time.*

8 The June 1993 issue of the *Washington Times* Volume *World and I* states that the energy generated by wind turbines in California can power all the residences of San Francisco; Darrell Dodge, 'Wind Power Rising,' *The World and I* 8 no. 6 (June 1993, 190).

9 Individualized services are witnessing a virtual explosion of activity, in both Canada and the United States. Sites are in operation in several provinces and in over 30 states. Several states, including Alaska, Oregon, Vermont, and Virginia, have legislatively mandated individualized services, in some instances creating the flexible funds required from out of the dollars that would have sent the child to residential treatment. For an overview of individualized services, see L. Adlai Boyd, 'Integrating Systems of Care for Children and Families: An Overview of Values, Methods and Characteristics of Developing Models, with Examples and Recommendations' (Tampa, Fla.: Department of Child and Family Studies, Florida Mental Health Institute, University of South Florida, July 1992); Judith W. Katz-Leavy, Ira S. Lourie, Beth A. Stroul, and Chris Zeigler-Dendy, 'Individualized Services in a System of Care' (Washington, DC: CASSP Technical Assistance Center, Center for Child Health and Mental Health Policy, Georgetown University Child Development Center, July 1992); and John D. Burchard, Sara D. Burchard, Robert Sewell, and John VanDenBerg, 'One Kid at a Time: A Case Study Evaluation of the Alaska Youth Initiative Demonstration Project' (Washington, DC: CASSP Technical Assistance Center, Center for Child Health and Mental Health Policy, and Georgetown University Child Development Center, August 1993). In terms of the structure of control, in many instances parents act as their own case managers.

10 Some of the examples described here are taken from a television special produced by the Canadian Broadcasting Corporation (CBC) entitled 'Trading Futures: Living in the Global Economy,' special report with David Suzuki, which aired on 4 April 1993.

11 See, for example, Daly's *Steady State Economics* (Washington, DC: Island Press 1991).

12 Netherlands Scientific Council for Government Policy, *Beleidsgerichte Toekomstverkenningen: Deel 2: Een Verruiming van Perspectief* (A Policy-Oriented Survey of the Future: Towards a Broader Perspective) (The Hague: Staatsuitgeverij 1983). An extensive English summary is available from the Council at Plein 1813, nr. 2, 2514 JN, The Hague.

13 Netherlands Scientific Council for Government Policy, *De Grenzen en*

Mogelijkheden van het Economisch Stelsel in Nederland (The Limits and Possibilities of the Economic System in Holland) (The Hague: Staatsuitgeverij 1983).

14 Ibid, 105.

CHAPTER 6: Sustainable Development

1 Quoted in Gerald Vandezande, *Christians in the Crisis* (Toronto: Anglican Book Centre 1984), 47.

2 Ibid.

3 Ibid.

4 In *Earth in the Balance* (New York: Houghton Mifflin 1992), 346, Al Gore calls for changing 'the definition of the GNP ... to include environmental costs and benefits.' And he minces no words: 'There is no excuse for not changing the definition of the GNP' (338).

5 Independent Commission of the South on Development Issues, *The Challenge to the South* (Oxford: Oxford University Press 1990).

6 Ibid, 279.

7 Ibid.

8 Mihajlo Mesarovic and Eduard Pestel, *Mankind at the Turning Point* (New York: Dutton 1974), 69.

9 Cited in B. Goudzwaard and H.M. de Lange, *Genoeg van te veel, Genoeg van te weinig: wissels omzetten in de economie*, 103.

10 As cited in the World Council of Churches, *Christian Faith and the World Economy Today* (Geneva: WCC Publications 1992), 18.

11 Nicholas A. Robinson, ed, *Agenda 21 and the UNCED Proceedings* (New York: Oceana Publications 1992).

12 As reported in Gary Gallon, 'Environmental Industries: Part of the New Canadian Economy,' *Jobs and the Environment: National Round Table Review* (fall 1993), 9.

13 World Council of Churches, *Christian Faith.*

14 World Council of Churches, *Accelerated Climage Change: Sign of Peril, Test of Faith* (Geneva: WCC Publications 1994).

CHAPTER 7: 'But That's Impossible!'

1 John Maurice Clark, *Studies in the Economics of Overhead Costs* (Chicago: University Press 1923).

2 We note that this argument is also easily made within the Round Tables on Environment and Economy. For example, in 'International Trade and

Sustainable Development: Dangers and Opportunities,' *Jobs and the Environment: National Round Table Review* (fall 1993), 32, Pierre-Marc Johnson and André Beaulieu espouse a classic post-care economic orientation when they write: 'In fact, free trade and the economic growth it brings are necessary for creating wealth, which in turn is essential to rectify past destruction of the environment. Simply stated, growth is essential for proper environmental restoration and remediation.'

3 The report appeared in November 1991.

4 Bread for the World Institute on Hunger and Development, *Hunger 1992* (Washington, DC, 1991), 34.

5 In *Earth in the Balance* (New York: Houghton Mifflin 1992), 313, Al Gore describes a population growth 'success story': 'one of the most interesting case studies of demographic transition in the Third World comes from the Kerala province of southwestern India, where population growth has stabilized at zero even though per capita incomes are still extremely low. The provincial leaders, with assistance from international population funding, developed a plan that is keyed to Kerala's unique cultural, social, religious, and political characteristics and focuses on a few crucial factors. First, they have achieved an extremely high rate of literacy, especially among women. Second, through good health care and adequate nutrition, they have lowered their infant mortality dramatically. And third, they have made birth control readily and freely available. The consequences are little short of remarkable: in an area of the world characterized by uncontrollable population growth, Kerala's rate more nearly resembles that of Sweden than nearby Bombay.'

6 Ibid, 187.

7 Feitse Boerwinkel, *Inclusief Denken: een Andere Tijd Vraagt een Ander Denken* (Inclusive Thinking: A Different Age Demands Different Thinking), 18th edition (Bussum: Unieboek 1975), first published in 1966.

8 In Martin Luther King, Jr, *A Testament of Hope: The Essential Writings of Martin Luther King Jr.*, ed James Melvin Washington (San Francisco: Harper & Row 1986), 625.

9 Ibid, 625

10 George Grant, *Lament for a Nation: The Defeat of Canadian Nationalism* (Ottawa: Carleton University Press 1989), first published 1965, x.

CHAPTER 8: A Twelve-Step Program for Economic Recovery

1 Years ago, the German philosopher Ernst Bloch wrote about Christians: 'When you begin to pay in hard cash for what you have preached about

– the poor, the exploited and the oppressed – then you are Christians. If you do not, then you are chatter-boxes and hypocrites.' Can we achieve something of the radicality of human action to which the Bible calls us, also in economics? Does not the call to conversion in today's context include a call for societal transformation? Has not the economy as it currently operates had a devastating impact on Christianity?

It is our conviction that the Christian community has paid too little attention to these questions. Perhaps the tension between the reality of life and the reality of God is so poignant that we hastily resign ourselves to doing something different on Monday than what we have committed ourselves to on Sunday.

2 Economist A.B. Cramp of Cambridge University was the first to use the metaphor of a 'tunnel society,' supported by a 'tunnel vision,' to describe our society. See A.B. Cramp, *Notes towards a Christian Critique of Secular Economic Theory* (Toronto: Institute for Christian Studies 1975), 62.

3 Quoted from an unpublished text of an address given in Toronto on 15 February 1993, at a conference entitled 'Beyond Foodbanks,' 11–12.

4 George Goyder, *The Responsible Company* (Oxford: Basil Blackwell 1961), and *The Just Enterprise* (London: A. Deutsch 1987).

5 Robert Bellah et al., *Habits of the Heart: Individualism and Commitment in American Life* (Berkeley: University of California Press 1985), 290.

6 Ibid, 290.

7 The working paper, from the Fiscal Policy and Economic Analysis Branch of Canada's Department of Finance, is by Louis Beauséjour, Gordon Lenjosek, and Michael Smart, entitled *An Environmental CGE Model of Canada and the United States*, Working Paper No. 92-04, ii. See also the 'economic instruments' investigations under way under the auspices of the National Round Table on the Environment and the Economy (as reported, for example, in the fall 1993 issue of the *National Round Table Review, Jobs and the Environment: Sustaining Canada's Future*), as well as the Ontario Fair Tax Commission's *Discussion Paper: Searching for Fairness*, a 1993 report commissioned by the Ontario Ministry of Finance.

8 See especially Beauséjour, Lenjosek, and Smart, *An Environmental CGE Model*. Using their computational model, the authors especially explore the effectiveness of a carbon tax in helping to reach the CO_2 emission standards that Canada agreed to in the Bergen Declaration. Based on their findings, they observe (55): 'It is said that regulation provides little or no incentive for firms to reduce pollution by more that the required emission standard. Market instruments, on the other hand, are seen as providing a continuous and dynamic incentive for firms to implement

new technologies and processes to control pollution if their cost is less than the cost implied by the economic instruments' (54). They conclude: 'In pursuing a particular environmental policy objective, it is shown that an economic policy instrument can succeed significantly, although indirectly, in achieving multiple environmental objectives' (55).

9 Ontario Round Table on Environment and Economy, *Restructuring for Sustainability* (Toronto 1992), 20; Ontario Fair Tax Commission, *Discussion Paper*, 94–6.

10 *Creating Opportunity: The Liberal Plan for Canada*, 64. See also the Department of Finance's *Final Report of the Task Force on Economic Instruments and Disincentives to Sound Environmental Practices* (Ottawa, November 1994).

11 Citizens for Public Justice, a Canada-wide organization of people seeking to promote justice in Canada's public affairs, called for this during the most recent federal election campaign. See its *Political Service Bulletin*, 'Getting Our House in Order' (Toronto: Citizens for Public Justice 1993), 6.

12 By and large, the fiscal involvement of the Canadian government has encouraged agribusiness and high levels of production at the expense of sustainability and stewardship. The issues, of course, are complex. But in keeping with what we have found in the overall economics-of-enough scenario, this alteration in incentive structure may also increase local independence and decision-making power and reduce the government's fiscal involvement in agriculture over time. Organizations such as the Christian Farmers Federation of Ontario have called for 'de-coupling' government price supports from specific commodities, in the belief that the present linkage encourages maximum production at the expense of sustainability and stewardship.

13 The Liberal party's platform, *Creating Opportunity*, contains several elements of the proposals outlined here. The platform adopts (66) the prevention principle: 'In the past, environmental policy has focused on managing and controlling the release of pollutants entering the environment. This approach has had only limited success. Canada needs a new approach that focuses on preventing pollution at its source. ... There is no alternative if Canadians wish to stop long-term pollutants from entering our air, soil, and water. A Liberal government will use the upcoming five-year review of the Canadian Environmental Protection Act to make pollution prevention a national goal and strengthen the enforcement of federal pollution standards.'

With respect to development of environmentally clean technologies and purification of waste gases and water, the platform states (66–7): 'A Liberal government will commit 25 percent of all new government funding for research and development to technologies that substantially reduce the harmful effects of industrial activity on the environment, or that specifically enhance the environment.' In addition, 'A Liberal government would assist provincial, regional, and municipal governments to finance new or renewed municipal sewage and water treatment infrastructure.' The platform also calls (68–9) for a broad educational effort.

14 *National Round Table Review*, 'Environmental NGOs in the 1990s' (spring 1993).

15 Herman E. Daly and Bernard B. Cobb, Jr, *For the Common Good* (Boston: Beacon Press 1989), 401–55.

16 As described, for example, in Daniel Blake Rubenstein, 'Full-Cost Accounting: Opportunities and Risk,' *National Round Table Review* (fall 1993), 22–3.

17 Gerald Vandezande, 'Too Much Poverty or Too Much Wealth?' *Toronto Star* 27 July 1993.

18 E.F. Schumacher, *Small Is Beautiful* (London: Abacus 1974).

19 Ibid, 123.

20 Ibid, 156.

21 Amos J. Paeslee, ed, *International Governmental Organizations: Constitutional Documents*, 5 vols. (The Hague: Martinus Nijhoff 1974), I, 458.

22 Al Gore, *Earth in the Balance* (Boston: Houghton Mifflin 1992), 346–7.

Index